19 to 17

19 to 17

Nick Geale

Tablo Publishing
Melbourne Australia

First published in 2022 by Tablo Publishing.
Level 1, 41–43 Stewart St, Richmond VIC 3121
www.tablo.com

21 22 23 LSC 10 9 8 7 6 5 4 3 2 1

19 to 17

19 to 17 doesn't seem a lot. If you close your eyes it happens in a flash. When you open your eyes, it takes a lot longer.

I was brought home to Number 19 as a one week old, add another 52 years and I end up at number 17, next door.

The words "Should, Would or Could" are not written, they can not change anything!

What I have learnt along the way is "everyone" has a story, all it takes is to sit down and "listen!"

I know I will be Opening some "Old Wounds" writing this but I needed to get things off my Chest!

I'd appreciate if you can donate something towards Mental Health or try and understand it more.

This is my story, I have put lots of photos in as the research has helped me get through a tough period, so apologies in advance.

To my Dear Mother, Aunty Sandra and Amanda's Parents, sorry for the "swearing"!

These are my words, no one has critiqued it.

I hope you enjoy it?

1st Innings

EARLY DAYS:

It all started in the mid 50's when our parents met at Teachers College in Sydney. From courting, they soon got engaged and married at Enfield in 1958. Dad rode through Baulkham Hills on his bicycle with open paddocks back then. He reckons he road from Strathfield which was a good distance away. I'd like to confirm this, however Dad is now 89 and has early Dementia. He had a fair idea where he'd like to live and start a Family.

Charles Street is off Windsor Road, the last side road coming up to the iconic Bull and Bush Hotel. It was the corridor from Parramatta to the Hawkesbury back in the early 1800's and still is to this day. It is the pathway for all the new housing estates, Box Hill, Kellyville, Rouse Hill, The Ponds and many more.

Mum and Dad bought a large block of land and built a modest two bedroom home. Dad chose number "19" Charles Street because it was at the top of the hill and he thought better for drainage. Not long after moving in, Mum fell pregnant and their first child, David Michael Geale was born on 7th Feb 1961. As I am adding and tweaking to my story, my Brother's 60th Birthday was due in a few weeks, more on that later.

As both were School Teachers, Mum and Dad were always at home with us on school holidays. Looking back now, having them around in those early days were priceless. There are not too many professions that have the luxury of spending so much time with their children.

#19 Charles Street, Early 60's, notice the small trees! Now over 50 feet tall.

David's Christening 1961. My Grandmother, Tuccia is holding him; Mum is looking down. Don't you love the Gloves worn in those Days! Unfortunately David was to re-visit this very Church some 16 Years later, in very "Sad" Circumstances!

Charles St looking from Windsor Rd. #19 on RHS on top of the hill in the distance, taken mid to late 60's.

My father (left) holding Anthony and David standing. His Twin Brother John with Michelle and Philip. 1964/65

We were only five years apart.
David 5, Anthony 4, Justin 2 and I'm 6 months.

In the back of #19, approx 1969. Justin is pushing the
Wheelbarrow, Anthony is squatting and I am inside.

I was the youngest of four boys, David, Anthony and Justin. Anyone in this category knows what it means to be last in line. I was always getting all the "hand be down" clothes, bikes, toys etc. When there was a wrestle going on, yours truely always came off second best. If I "dobbed" on my Brothers, they always put it in their memory bank. I had to grow up quickly!

My earliest memory was when I went to Kindergarten near the park at the bottom of Charles Street. I was four and a bit at the time and remember screaming when Mum dropped me off on my first day. Unfortunately I only lasted two days and my Uncle came to pick me up because Mum was teaching.

Mum taught at the Public Primary School, not too far from our home called Baulkham Hills Primary. She eventually ended up teaching in the Library and coincidentally Dad too did the same. He taught a little further away at Seven Hills West Primary.

Baulkham Hills Primary School, these are the only buildings left, now Residential Units.

They both were big readers and took this passion towards teaching the kids. If it wasn't reading books to the younger ones, it was about research and navigating their way around the library. They both had creative minds and finding a topic sometimes daily was invaluable to the students.

If any of us were sick, Dad took us into his School. Being there was a bit weird as we were either similar age or a bit older. Dad was quite strict, in a way no different to home. If anyone was playing up, he was happy to bring out the ruler. He'd ask the student in trouble to put their hand on the table. "Whack", he missed their hand on purpose and hit the table. It was all about whose Boss and Dad seemed to win over the Students.

Roll onto year 2015. I had a Business near Windsor and next door there was a Plywood Shop. Dave who owned it had a mate helping out, his name was Borgy. One day I had a bit of time to kill and I popped in to say G'Day. I asked them, "how did you both meet" and they said, "we went to the same Primary School". Naturally I asked "where"? To my surprise they said "Seven Hills West". I replied, "Bullshit"!

I asked them, "do you remember Mr Geale"? They said "yeh, he was the Librarian" I said, "he is my Father"! They were both totally shocked and story after story with lots of laughing. Dave is on Facebook with the Ex Students of Seven Hills West and I sent him a photo of my elderly Father. He posted Dad's photo and it didn't take long before numerous Ex Students replied. Here are a few of their comments.

- So many of his good traits have left imprints in our lives, I'm sure.

- This is where my love of books came from.

- He has left so many of us students with fond memories. I don't remember all the teachers but Mr Geale in the library, lives on forever.

- I think every student from Seven Hills West remember'd your Dad. He had an impact on so many students in a good way. Cherish the time you have left with your Dad.

- Oh Mr Geale, my favourite time at school was being a library monitor. Best times I loved, was being in the library and have always loved reading. I always had so much respect for you. Thinking of you.

- To the Man that taught me to Love reading and books.

- This is great that such one person, a Teacher for us all made such a difference.

- Still have fond memories of your Library and discovering new books.

- Such fond Memories of you and spending time in the Library, my favourite place at School.

- Fond Memories of you and the Library, especially the book bus!

- Such a cruel disease. No wonder you are so proud of him when he is so fondly remembered.

I only wish Dad was Mentally with us as he'd love to hear and read all these beautiful comments.

*Dad's Retirement Day, 1st July 1992, Seven Hills West
Primary, presented by Elaine Lowrey*

Dad was also a health freak and always carried a handkerchief. He was paranoid if anyone sneezed near him. I still remember him lining up the students visiting the Library. He'd ask them individually as they got to him,"show me your handkerchief". If they didn't have one, he'd role some toilet paper off and hand it to them. I have multiple posts from Ex Students commenting about his hygiene. This has rubbed off on me and to this day I always carry a hanky!

Mum took me under her wing at her school. My memories were few, drinking milk in the small bottles every day and wearing a dark grey uniform. I also remember hearing the big explosions from the road being constructed in the bush close by. It is now the pathway from Baulkham Hills to North Rocks. There was also an awkward moment with me having the "runs" in the toilet block but Mrs Geale came to the rescue!

My first school, 1st Grade aged 4.

My Brothers were just up the road in the Catholic School, Our Lady of Lourdes. When I was old enough I joined them in 2nd Class, not Year 2 as it's known today. I quickly made friends with Pes, Macca, Ando and Blacky. We all played soccer and footy most lunchtimes and was always very competitive. It got a bit interesting when the ball went across the busy Windsor Road. The Teacher on duty had to go and fetch the ball, dodging in and out of any traffic.

Photo taken on the grounds we played soccer and footy.

Sister Angela was the Principal and she was very strict. I still remember getting the feather duster on my backside. Dad gave us the strap but the feather duster handle hurt so much more! I was a wild child and when I was in Fourth Class my teacher, Mrs Spithill moved me on to the other Fourth Class. Luckily, Mrs Campbell saved me from being thrown out!

When I reflect now in my 50's, I wonder why was I so disruptive at such a young age? I seemed to lap up the attention that maybe I was not getting as much at home? I grew up with an outgoing personality and this no doubt contributed to me getting into trouble.

Mum got involved at the School and ran the annual Fete. It was great going to each store and my favourite was the "hoopla". You were given about 10 hoops made of cane, approximately eight inches wide. You had to get the hoop totally around the prize to win it, great fun. The Chocolate Wheel was always a favourite with Macca and Blacky's Fathers mostly running it. They'd stand on top of a big truck trailer and spin the wheel with everyone in suspense. Towards the end of the day the prizes seemed to get smaller and smaller, oh well.

There was also an Art Show each year and was held in the old cottage located in the grounds of the School. I think this is where Mum got her fascination with Art. Without a doubt, every year there was a new addition to 19 Charles Street. Mum was so generous and even though deep down she knew funds were tight, an extra painting appeared. Mum understood the Artists were important and wanted to keep it a rolling event.

Young also meant I was extremely naïve. I distinctly remember putting some lead from a pencil in my ear. Luckily I told my Parents, so off to the Doctors. My Uncle heard I was at the Doctors. He was my hero, larger than life and a bit of a stirrer. He had a Paul Hogan personality and everything was a joke or a laugh. He brought my Brothers up to the Doctors and I still can recall them looking through the window laughing.

There was also another scary moment that I don't think I have shared with too many. I was in the kitchen by myself and the jug was boiling. It was a one of those flip lid ceramic ones with the element exposed. I dropped a biscuit in it and when it was still "on" I put my hand in the water to get the biscuit out. I got an "electric shock" and it scared the shit out of me. It was an extremely lucky escape!

Dad was a Father like no other! He was not the "Sporty Type" but had a great imagination to keep us interested. He took us to the Park with swings and slippery slides just down the road. He was more than happy to drive us anywhere to find a new Park to have fun! We have priceless footage of all four of us jumping out of Dad's old black Chev in a Park at Parramatta. We'd be running as fast as anything to be the first on the swings but I was more than happy to climb the stairs on the slide and hit the sand at the bottom.

*Dad with his 1936 Chev. The plates are still in the
Family! How good is my Old Man looking!*

His main adventure was to take us down to the local bush. We'd grab
the buckets and nets and all excited, off we'd go. Our main target was
catching skinks and Dad was the expert in helping us catch them. If
it was a hot day, they'd laze on the rocks asleep. We'd crawl up and
"bang", throw over our nets. I am not sure of our strike rate but hey it
was great fun.

Dad was quite handy with wood making and a lot of our toys we
played with were made by him. The toys he made were simple and we
shared them with each other. When I look back now, how lucky were
we to have a such a great Father.

One of our favourite games was dressing up in Cowboys and
Indians outfits. We'd chase each other around the back and front lawns
with guns drawn. Being four of us, we were so fortunate to just make
things up. Sitting on a simple boat swing or being pushed around in
the original bucket style wheel barrow with my Brothers was great
stuff. Being around them was so cool and I often think how lucky I was
to have three.

There was an ugly incident one day when we were out the front. For some reason, I had a pair of scissors with me and Anthony wanted them. I bolted towards the driveway with him chasing me. As I entered the front path, I threw them on the ground. Anthony did not see the scissors and stepped on them. They went from one side of his ankle and out the other! I vanished and hid somewhere inside. He eventually returned from the Hospital, all patched up and in good spirits.

Dad always took a few of us to Church which was generally 6 pm on a Sunday night. Someone normally hid in the small storage area located in the back of the VW beetle. After reversing the car and starting to drive off, he'd jump up and say, "I'm here"! No doubt Dad knew someone else was in the car as he had to pass the back to get in. I can only think like all Dads, he went along with the fun.

It was always a fight to see who sat in the passenger seat. The winner had the chance to steer the car leaning across. Dad always tried to avoid the lights and this common back road one day came back to haunt us, back to that later. At Church looking back now, was a way to keep the cattle calm. Maybe it was a ploy in Dad's eyes to give Mum an hour or so off from all the craziness?

We were so lucky when Mum & Dad decided on 19 Charles Street Baulkham Hills. Up the road at number 26 was the Dobson Family. There were five boys, Michael, Peter, John, Ken and Ben. We spent most of our early days crossing the road to each other's home. We'd normally play out all day in each other's back yard, unless it was raining.

The "Dobbos", as we use to call them had a large back yard and Cricket was the normal game under their Mulberry tree. We played all day and when it was getting late, Margaret stood on the balcony calling out, "you Geale boys, time to go home"!

Over the years they did up their backyard into a nice Grass Tennis court. It also turned into a good cricket pitch. Luckily, there were high wire fences that saved lots of tennis and cricket balls going into neighbouring backyards. Both families were extremely competitive and even when things heated up, there were never any punch ups.

Dobbos #26 and Geales #19. David and Michael are in Blue. Peter has a Hat on, Anthony is rubbing his eye and John is far right.

The main way of expressing our feelings was to hammer a sign into the front of each other's foot path. If we were not flavour of the day, the Dobson boys wrote on their sign saying, "Geale's Bard" and knock it in outside #26. If it was them, it read "Dobbo's Bard" and we'd knock it in outside #19. When our Parents arrived home or walked out the front and spotted the signs, no doubt they had a "chuckle"! Straight away peace making proceeded and next day we played again as if nothing ever happened.

We were the lucky ones with Mum and Dad deciding to put a pool in our backyard. I was aged 7 at the time and it became a great draw card for those hot days. Dad hated the pool as he wanted a Rugby motorcar instead but Mum won the battle. He rarely swam in it and begrudgingly cleaned it and maintained it for over 40 years.

*Dobbos and Geales having a Swimming Race. Justin
is wearing Brown shorts in the middle.*

We still however had a bit of yard left for a small Cricket Pitch. My Brother Justin use to hurl down the "six sticher" cricket ball. I was wearing no pads or gloves, it was terrifying. There was one day when I missed the ball and it crashed into the garage window. We retrieved the ball and kept playing on. Dad was ok and took him ages to replace that glass.

At age 7, Dad bought a cat for my birthday. It was sandy in colour, however as it came from a factory environment it had black grease and dust all over him. They decided to call him Sambo. Can you imagine in these new times using that word? As a kid I was far too young to understand what it meant.

Sambo loved sleeping on Mum and Dad's bed. If Sambo wasn't home before Dad went to bed, he'd walk around the house using a distinctive "calling" sound. Sambo somehow appeared and Dad took him in for the night. I was in my late teens when Sambo sadly passed away. Dad dug a hole out the back yard and we both buried him. It was really emotional for both of us, however a good Father and Son moment.

Dad and Sambo out the back of #19.

We were lucky that around the corner was a group of shops. The milk bar was our favourite owned by Mr Deep. We spent so much time playing the pin ball machine (pinnies) and Joe Deep also loved playing them with us. There was many a time we waited outside his shop as he cruised up Arthur Street in his station wagon. He normally went to the Wholesalers before opening up, nothing rushed him. We helped him with his supplies and got to play the "pinnies" quicker.

He sold lollies in a glass cabinet with no tongs in those days. Joe used his fingers and put the bananas, snakes and frogs into small paper bags. Today the shop is now a Chinese Take Away. When I tell them the story about the milk bar, they seem to struggle to understand the History of it all, oh well.

There was also an Antique Shop on the top corner and Dad was always visiting to see if there were any bargains. I think it helped him become interested in old radios and his Twin Brother John, with gramophones. At the back of the shops was a vacant block of land. We rode our bikes and if anyone was lucky enough to own a motor bike, we watched them ride.

Yattendon Oval, my place of "Solace". The "Swings" are in the same spot as we were kids with the only thing missing is the famous "Slippery Dip"! The hill in the Background is where we rode down and I also walked to School. I can still remember "Flying" my kite with my Dad. Directly behind the "Electrical" Post in the background was my "Pre School" for 2Days!

We mainly stayed local, Arthur St, Charles St or Yattendon Crescent where our local Park was. It was always so big to me being so young. It had a large hill surrounding one side and a Grandstand on the opposite side. We rode our bikes down the big hill or just rolled down it and after always itching ourselves. The greatest fun was riding the Billy Carts that Dad made. We started at the top of the lane way, speeding down the concrete path onto the grass and down the hill. There were no helmets in those days and you just hung on for grim death!

My other distant memory of Yattendon Oval was flying kites, once again that Dad made. He lied down on the hill with me and both looking up to the sky watching my kite. Life was simple in those days, no technology to distract you. At this Park was also the location of our School Sport Carnivals. We have "precious" footage of us running and more importantly David is in it!

I was a year older than Ken at #26 and I'd walk over to get him for School. He was never on time so I'd wait and we walked through the

Park as it was a short cut to School. Now I live up the road again, I regularly walk in the Park and the memories come flooding back.

STARTING YOUNG:

Work has always been a normal thing to me and it all started with my Uncle! He had a paper run and he'd turn up at the crack of dawn, car full of papers. In those days they were rolled up in plastic, making them easy to throw. Uncle Mike threw them over the roof, mostly landing in the correct driveway. My job was to select the correct paper, either the Sun, Mirror or Herald. When the run was done, it was back to the Newsagent. I ran up those stairs quickly as my payment for helping was a "Cherry Ripe" chocolate bar. To this day I still love them.

Mowing lawns was another line of work for him. When he needed a hand, he'd turn up and sometimes two of us went out for the day. He'd throw the "cut grass" on the back of his Ute and when we arrived for the next job, most of the grass was gone! Helping him, gave me the confidence to one day mow my Grandmother's lawn. I mostly rode my bike to her house which took about five minutes. I think I was about Ten, maybe Eleven and I was given a $2 note.

A great Pic of my Grandmother's home overlooking her backyard. It has been extended to a 2 Storey Home. The people who live there are the same who bought it after "Tuccia" passed away in 1988. The small metal fence is where we use to play in the underground pipes as kids! Taken 2021.

My Grandmother Tuccia outside her home, she
always had a "fag" in her hand!

She had a small home and I always had a glass of lemon cordial out of a schooner glass. She collected them when walking past the Bull and Bush. There is a story kicking about told by my Uncle. He was at the Pub one day and a few of his mates noticed an "old lady" collecting schooner glasses from the brick wall out the front of the Pub. My Uncle looked and said "shit, that's my Mother"!

As well as mowing her lawn, I use to clean here gutters from all the fallen gum leaves. I'd fill up the bin liners and throw them down to her with no ladders or safety harness used.

My Uncle also started another small business, making concrete steps. His first location was at the back of his Mother's house. We had to prepare the steel moulds by oiling them all over with just a sponge and no gloves. Next was the steel, normally done by Uncle Mike. The final job was to pour the concrete into them. We had to barrow the concrete from the front of my Grandmother's house and then along the path to the back. The empty moulds were lined up on timber stands, next a vibrating pad got all the concrete into all the gaps.

After a few days of drying, we had to undo all the nuts and take away the metal moulds, with nice new steps exposed. When pouring the concrete the front face of the step had small air holes. For the steps to look finished, we needed to fill the holes with cement using a sponge. We had to wipe the front all over and it took us a while getting it right but we soon got the knack of it.

Ok, time we really grew up, ready to deliver them. I was the youngest, so only allowed to lift the four foot steps. David being the eldest, had the strength to lift the five footers at the age of 13 or 14. I don't really know how heavy they were but in time, I was ready to pick up the five footers. We had to walk them to the Ute and stack them on the back and off to the building sites. We got it right most of the time, remembering no GPS in those days, just the traditional UBD Street Directory. Nearly 45 years later this style of step is still sold and no doubt a better more efficient method used.

His main line of work was driving a concrete truck. The original company he worked for was called Redimix. It was always exciting driving around with him as he'd honk his horn to the kids if they waved as we passed them. The last company was Boral and he was one of the longest serving drivers in NSW. I went to his Surprise Leaving Party that was arranged by his work mates. He finished up in his early 70's.

FAMILY:

To help pay school fees my Father joined the Army Reserves. He was employed as a Pay Clerk and also took it upon himself as chief tea maker. His work place was Victoria Barracks, right next to the Old Sydney Show Ground and SCG. It was very handy when the Show was on, with free parking and more importantly without the hassle of finding a spot.

It was always exciting driving up to the Guard Box and seeing the Soldier with his rifle and in uniform. Dad mostly wore a beret at work, although he had the classic slouch hat if he was in a Parade. He still wears a beret almost every day, which has become synonymous to him.

Dad went on a Camp every second year, two weeks from memory. It was when we became more mischievous and no doubt a handful for Mum. She was out one night, so David grabbed the slug gun and started shooting at cars driving past. He also shot Anthony in his foot, asking him to "dance "on the tiled patio. It was a good 10/15 years later, a slug was taken out of his foot!

Dad was always interested in the Army as his father was an original ANZAC who served in the 1st World War. Thomas Geale was a member of the 1st Light Horse Regiment, AIF. He was wounded at Gallipoli. My Grandad's (PaPa's) "exact" wording.

"I landed at Gallipoli at 10.30 am on the 11th May 1915. Wounded on the 19th May, 0400 hours and was transferred to hospital at Valletta in Malta- 22 May 1915. (Wounds-3, bullet wounds right arm; 1 chest bullet wound)".

He came back home to Australia and went back on a Second Tour in Aug 1917. He arrived in Messines France, 9th Nov 1917, his words. "Battle of Hill 60. I was wounded by the explosion of a German 5-9 shell which destroyed the field piece and killed the rest of the gun crew".

"I received wounds to both arms and right hip as well as shell shock. My uniform was blasted from me and a piece of shell casing tore through my left breast pocket, cutting through my wallet and a number of photographs".

"This thick wallet saved my life! A soldier picked up the damaged pieces from the mud. An officer had continually stressed the importance of packing the left breast pocket". "The remains of this wallet and contents are still in existence. The wounding occurred on the eleventh hour on the eleventh day of the eleventh month, 1917".

My Grandfather's items from 1st World War. Picture of his Mother cut into a biscuit; a ration biscuit and the note pad/ wallet that saved his life with the hole created by shrapnel.

Luckily we have the small wallet in the family with some mud on it as mentioned above. One day I will contact the War Memorial in Canberra to see if they think worth exhibiting? We are very fortunate to have a folder full of photos and stories from his Service that my Uncle John researched. As a child you never really understood the sacrifices that our Service Men and Women made for us!

Getting back to the Sydney Show or the Easter Show. Dad took us every year and the highlight was definitely the Showbag Hall. We were spoilt rotten and it was all about how many bags we got. They were the paper ones, not the plastic ones today. We also went on the rides and always visited the big Hall that displayed the fruit. It was fascinating seeing how big the displays were. I use to think, how clever they were to show off the themes so clearly. Lets not forget the animal section with chooks, ducks, cows, plus many more. It always had that Farm smell about it, unlike the environment we grew up in.

The only time we ever experienced a farm was when Dad took us to Murrundia. It is located in the Hunter Valley. It was a happy place for him as it was his first placement as a young School Teacher. We camped in a tent and he took his rifle and showed us how to fire it. Dad had a friend up in Murrundia, his name was Doug Ireland. Apparently Dad helped Doug build his house and only recently when I referred to Doug Ireland, although as I mentioned earlier he has dementia, he replied to helping him build his house!

Mum and her family spent a lot of their young lives in a town called Greta, not a long way from Murrundia. The reason they were drawn to Greta was my Grandad, Nino Gremmo. He secured a job as Head Wool Classifier at Burlington Mills, about a 10 minute bus ride from their home. He brought over these qualifications from Europe and luckily he found employment.

They lived at a little place called Harpers Hill on the old New England Hwy. Opposite was a dairy farm and Uncle Mike use to swim in the dam on the property. In the distance was the Greta Camp, located just behind the railway line. When going to the Camp, my Mum, Brother and Sister took empty buckets with them. As a train went past, the workers on the train threw coal out and they loaded their buckets up and took them home for the fire.

Greta is well known for the Army Camp from 1939-1949. It was used to house and train the Military in readiness for combat. It was also used to house the Migrants from Europe from 1949-1960. My Grandad was a Linguist and he worked part time at the Camp teaching English to the new migrants. He spoke several Languages including his Native Italian, French, Russian, Yugoslavian and German. He also managed to teach himself Japanese and Spanish. Going to the Court House in Maitland was a normal event if any of the newcomers needed assistance and he'd go with them as their interpreter.

*Greta Migrant Camp.1949-1960. My Uncle, Aunty
and Mother visited the Camp regularly.*

*Greta Camp. The old bricks were from the original accommodation.
Look carefully in the background, one of the huts used.*

My Mother and her Sister went to the Catholic Girls School named St Joseph's in Lochinvar, about a 5 min bus ride. My Uncle went to Marist Brothers in Maitland, a bit further on. My Grandad moved away to Mount Isa in North Queensland to chase better employment. Not long after he arrived, he wrote to my Grandmother asking her to leave Greta and reunite the family to Mt Isa. Nino called his wife Tuccia after an ancient Roman Vestal Virgin. She declined the offer, as she wanted her children to finish their Schooling in the Hunter.

He dug his heals in and stayed in Mt Isa, living a single Man's life. When he returned back to Sydney in the late 70's he was nothing like the Man he was. I still remember him getting out of the car at #19 and Mum walking to him and hugging her Daddy! It was the first time my Mum had seen him for over 20 years.

He was housed in a Retirement Village near Austral, not to far away from the City of Liverpool. I can remember going to visit him, I was about 10 at the time. Not long after he arrived, he was admitted to Hospital and I went to see him with Mum. The memory I have is seeing my Grandad all hooked up with small pipes and leads. He sadly died not long after, mainly due to alcoholism, he was not quite 65.

COUSINS:

We spent a lot of time with our Cousins growing up. There's four boys, Michael, Andrew, Richard, David and the youngest is Melissa. They lived only ten minutes away and yes Dad always went a back way to drop us off. When we were old enough we rode our bikes via the route Dad always took. Uncle Mike and Aunty Elaine let us stay for tea and more then likely we slept over. They too had a pool and in the Summer, if we were not swimming we'd be playing cricket. We never spent much time inside, only to have lunch and a drink then back outside to have fun.

There was an interesting moment one day when we were playing softball on the front lawn. From memory, David hit the ball straight through our Uncle and Auntie's bedroom window. Everyone scattered except for young Michael and we were all petrified that our Uncle may have gone crazy.

I was the closest to them in age and they were like 2nd Brothers to me. None of us ever fell out and to this day we get on so well. They often visited Charles Street and one day Aunty Elaine walked into the kitchen and asked my Mum, "hey Elsa, where are the boys"? My Mum's reply was, "probably on the roof" and carried on with her cooking! Imagine that today!

Dad in #19 Family Room with my Cousins, Andrew and David the youngest. Dad was always on the floor playing games with all the children in his Family! He was Unique! Notice the Happy Days Pin Ball machine .

Every Christmas Eve, Uncle Mike turned up and everyone jumped on the back of his Ute. He drove around the streets, honking his horn with us all singing songs like, "Jingle Bells, Jingle Bells and You Better Watch out, You Better Not Cry, Santa Claws is Coming To Town".

Aunty Sandra, Mum's sister, lived in Bathurst past Lithgow. They moved there because her Husband was transferred as he worked for Telecom, now called Telstra. There were three girls, Michaela, Gemma, Natasha and a boy, Mathew. Every Christmas they came down and stayed at Charles Street or at my Uncle and Auntie's house. Christmas with all three families together was so much fun.

Christmas 1988, it's a special photo as 4 years later Aunty
Elaine sadly passed away due to Breast Cancer. She
is in the middle sitting down with dark hair.

Uncle Peter unfortunately developed Polio as a young man. He use to hobble up the side of our house using a walking stick and later years in a wheelchair. He took a liking to me as I played cricket and he and I chatted about the Test Series being played at the time.

HIGH SCHOOL:

From Primary School, Our Lady of Lourdes, we all went to a High School called Oakhill College. We use to catch the bus at the top of our road, it took about 20 minutes. My older Brothers always seemed to be in trouble. My eldest David was expelled and it was off into the big wide world for him, more on that later. We wore a Blazer in the winter months as well as a tie. Luckily in the Summer months, shorts and only a collard short sleeve shirt.

In my Oakhill College Uniform outside #19, Year 1978.

My first thoughts of High School was how strict it was. The "strap" was the normal method of discipline. If you got "six of the best" you were considered tough! I was always asked regularly to "pull my socks up" by one particular Brother Michael. As I looked around, there were heaps of other kids with their socks down and I was sure he had my name marked.

I still remember the first day in 6th Class. We were talking about the States of Australia and our Teacher asked a question, "does anyone know what Interstate means"? I put my hand up and said, "it means in the State". She berated me and said, "you will end up going back to 5th Class if your not careful"! Bitch!

When I got off the bus one day, Pes came up to me on the "Bull Paddock" and he said, "Elvis Presley died"! My reply was, "who's that"? He was blown away and still to this day when it comes up, he takes the piss out of me. Music has never been a big part of my life and I sometimes ask myself why? Maybe it was because Mum and Dad never had music playing at home. My eldest brother David liked Music and in a few Chapters it will make sense that he never was allowed to pass his love onto me.

There was an Agricultural Department at School and my Brother Anthony loved being with the animals. He convinced our Parents into buying a horse. His name was Midnight as he was black in colour. He was an old horse and normally had a placid personality. I rode him one day and he bolted towards the fence and I hung on tight and luckily he slowed down, once was enough!

One day Anthony decided to ride Midnight home to Charles Street which was a good 15 miles away. When he arrived home my Mum took a photo of all four boys and Midnight. I was sitting on him and my Brother David was showing off, pushing his cigarettes up a little higher in his pocket for the photo. None of us knew how significant this photo was!

I am sitting on Midnight, Justin is holding the rope, Anthony is leaning on Midnight and David in Blue. Year 1977.

It was too late to ride Midnight back to School, so he stayed in our backyard for the night. The next day we tried to walk him out which developed into a problem. For some reason he didn't want to walk up the small railway sleeper stairs. We tried everything, until George our back neighbour popped his head over the back fence and said, "put some sand on the steps". We took his advice and Midnight walked straight up them. Anthony jumped on and he rode back to School. This area out the back was where a photo was taken by my Mum one day. I was holding my first cricket bat, I was about 5/6 years of age. I still remember buying it at a small Sports shop located in the arcade in Baulkham Hills. I was the only one who took cricket up in the family as all the others played Rugby League and went to the beach in the Summer. More about cricket, my passion later.

TRAGEDY:

There was a fruit shop up the road owned by the Bombardier family. I am not sure how we made the connection but my Brother David was the first of the Geale boys to work there. Their Farm was down near the end of Arthur Street, where most of the veggies were grown. There was also another Farm only two minutes away up the hill. David quickly developed a close friendship with the Italian Brothers. They were all car freaks and David became more interested in them too.

Old Shops at Baulkham Hills near the small park where we got off the Bus and walked to the Fruit Shop. The Green Sign on the roof is where the Fruit Shop was. Taken July 2021

As well as working in the fruit shop, David took up a Mechanical

Apprenticeship. Michael Dobson, the eldest at number 26 Charles Street also took on the same trade. Jim his Father, was the General Manager at Cullens Nissan dealership at Concord. We have some brief footage of David working there, once again priceless.

It was decided that the boys needed a car to drive each other to work with both Parents paying half each. The car was garaged at our house and when Dad was away on Camp, David use to take it for Joy Rides without a Licence. This was always kept a secret from my Father.

David at the Fruit Shop, not long before he passed away.

It was an early Friday evening and my Dad arrived home after visiting his Father in the Nursing Home at Eastwood. He discovered the little Cortina missing from the garage. It was then my Father realised what had been going on. We had an inkling where David might be, that being Willy's house, one of the Bombardarie's.

I was in the car, so was my Brother Anthony. As we were reversing out the driveway, Michael was walking from across the road. He asked "where are you going?" We replied,"finding David" and Michael too jumped in the car. As we arrived outside Willy's house located in between the two farms, our gut feel was confirmed. I can vividly remember seeing David in the garage, little did I know it was the last time I set eyes on him!

Michael jumped out first as he had his licence and was "suppose" to drive the car back home. Anthony too jumped out and I was just about to but my Dad said "no you stay here with me"! Not long after we got home, the phone rang. Dad answered it and I think it was Michael saying, "there has been an accident"! Dad and Jim, Michael's Father, both drove down to the accident scene. It was Huxley Drive Winston Hills, the road we used to go to Church as I mentioned earlier.

The last time I saw my Brother David, he was standing in this garage on that Night!

We learnt later that the car rolled over with David who demanded to drive and not wearing a seatbelt. Luckily Michael was wearing his seat belt and somehow Anthony survived, literally holding on for grim death under the back seat. Dad returned from the accident scene and he was standing in the kitchen and I will never forget his words, "expect the worst"! His mouth was quivering and I started to cry and although I was quite young, I knew how serious the situation was!

We went over to the Dobsons and I can still remember their Grandmother was there as well as all the family, except Jim and Michael. I stayed there for a while until Uncle Mike arrived and he carried me up their drive. We headed back to his place and I slept in their bed. I still can recall the "screech" of the tyres as Uncle Mike sped away to the hospital.

My Father, Mother, Jim and Michael from #26 as well as Anthony went to the Hospital and Uncle Mike arrived a bit later. Jim's words, "We sat down in the small meeting room and they offered us coffee and biscuits and I knew then it was Serious! The Doctor came in and said, "we need to take your Son off "Life Support" as he has terrible brain injuries"! Elsa agreed that this is best for David and it to be turned off".

David's Memorial Card.

I was listening to Jim on the way home after we visited Dad on his 89th Birthday in the Nursing Home. I said, to Jim as I was driving, "wasn't that a bit weird that you stayed with Mum and not Dad". He said "your Mum thought it was best that Harold was with Michael and Anthony

as the accident was only a few hours before and take them home".
"Your Mum had accepted the fact that she lost David and I stayed with
Elsa until it was turned off and drove her home".

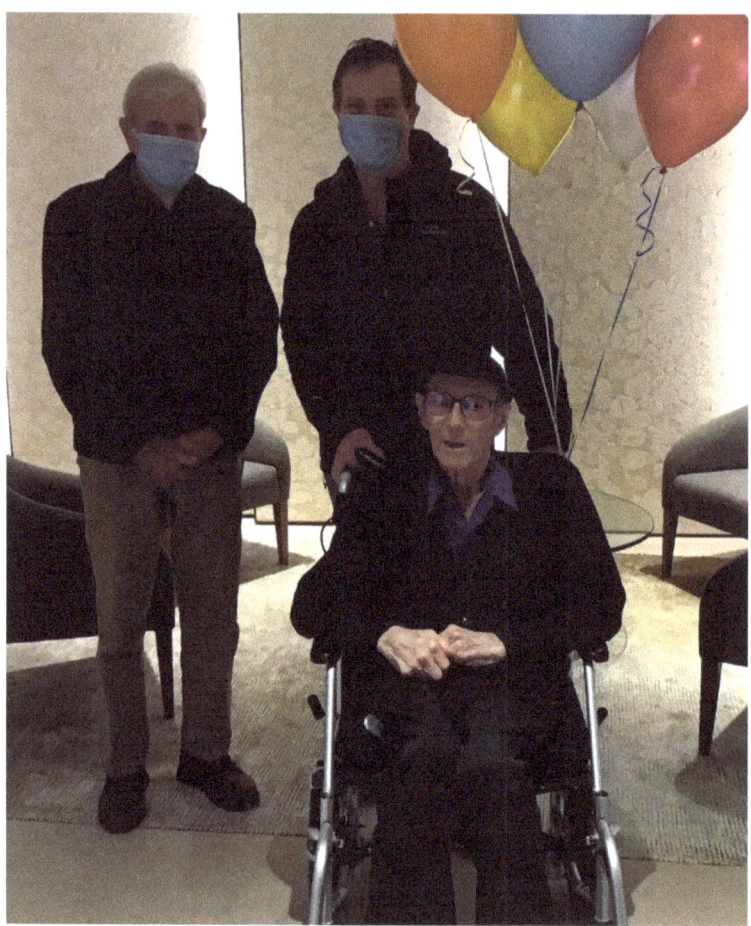

*Jim from #26 and Me visited Dad on 1st July 2021 on his 89th
Birthday. Sadly Dad didn't know either of us, due to his Dementia!*

I woke up in the morning and walked into my Aunty and Uncle's
lounge room. Aunty Elaine gave me a hug and said, "David has gone to
heaven"! The Date was 6th August 1977. It was a Saturday and to keep
me busy, I still went to watch my School Rugby Team play. I remember

talking to Mr Hillman and I told him "my Brother had died last night", he was already informed.

I arrived back home and still remember sitting in our back family room watching TV with my other two Brothers. There was a knock on the door and one of the Bombardier's delivered a big box of fruit. I was protected from the gravity of the night before and I never ever witnessed my Parents crying, which I thought was weird as I got older.

My small memory of the Funeral were the School kids standing on both sides of the driveway into the Church. I can recall seeing Peter Dobson crying in the Church and our back neighbour Liz was in tears too, not much more. There was no "counselling" in those days, so us three boys just sort of got on with it. I was just 11 years of age, Justin was nearly 13 and Anthony was 15. Mum and Dad were in their Forties and Mum became the rock in our home!

Going away on a Holiday was extremely rare to us. Mum and Dad decided after David died that we all go away up the Central Coast to Wamberal Beach, just outside Terrigal. It was good fun riding our body boards, made of tough rubber and slippery as. Dad was not a beach person, so him being with us was a treat and are lucky to have some footage of our stay.

One of my distinct memories was watching Australia vs West Indies in the World Series Cricket on a black and white TV. It was the 1st year, 77/78 Season played at VFL Park in Melbourne. The Windies needed a Six of the last ball and the bowler was Mick Milone with Wayne Daniel facing. Milone bowled the ball and Daniel smashed it for Six into the Grandstand to Win. It was then my passion of Cricket was confirmed!

My Brother Justin and I went to an early WCC game at the Sydney Show Ground as Games were not allowed to be played on the SCG. It was Australia vs West Indies. We were literally next to the boundary rope behind the slips. Any cricket lovers out there will remember the "classic" catch that went to the slips and was fumbled, landed on the keeper's foot and was eventually caught. I still remember the shouts of "catch, catch" by the slips and keeper and the players involved were Clive Lloyd, Derek Murray but can not recall the third?

It was not until a good 30 or so years later that I noticed we were part of an iconic TV Commercial. Let me try and give you a hint.

"Lillee's pounding down like a machine,

"Pascoe's making diverts in the green,

"Marshy's taking wickets,

"Hooksy's clearing pickets,

"And the Chappell eye's has got that killer clean,

"C'mon Aussie C'mon C'mon,

"C'mon Aussie C'mon C'mon,

"Mr Walker playing havoc with the batsman,

"Redpath it's good to see you back,

"Lairdy's making runs,

"And Dougies chewing gum,

"And Gilmores willing willow like an axe,

"C'mon Aussie C'mon C'mon, "C'mon Aussie C'mon C'mon,

Quite early on the Ad, there were a few boys jumping up and down and it took me a few times watching it to realise that my Brother and I were in the Commercial.

World Series Cricket 1977 TV Commercial. I am the skinny one with white hat and my Brother Justin is in Blue.

World Series Cricket Aussie Team. Pic is on the back
of a small Vinyl Record with the Theme Song, C'mon
Aussie C'mon. This Song "Saved" Kerry Packer.

Back Row: *Dennis Lille, Martin Kent, Ray Bright, David Hookes,*
Richie Robinson, Max Walker, Ian Redpath, Kerry O'Keeffe.
Middle Row: *Rick McCosker, Garth McKenzie, Wayne Prior, Ashley*
Mallett, Len Pascoe, Mick Malone, Ian Davis, Gary Gilmore.
Front Row: *Trevor Chappell, Doug Walters, Greg Chappell,*
Ian Chappell, Rod Marsh, Bruce Laird, Ross Edwards.

Holding my 1st Cricket Bat. Head and Stance is
Good, need to work on my Grip! Aged 6.

In those days we played over two weekends and at the finish of a game on the first week, luckily I was not out. The following Saturday I continued batting and scored my first ever Century! It was suggested that I go and try out for the Rep team. I was a bit shocked but I thought why not. It was the start of getting serious and I made the Northern Districts Moore Shield team.

We played the Final at North Sydney Oval and it was the first time any of us had played on a Turf Pitch. We bowled first and Gavin Robertson was opening the bowling. Their opener David Nui was a left hander and he nicked one and I dove to my left and caught him.

It was a moment that I have never forgotten. Years later I brought it up with Nuiy, who now lives in the States.

1979-80 NORTHERN DISTRICTS   MOORE   SHIELD TEAM.

BACK ROW. ANDREW HEMMINGS. IAN MATTHEWS. GAVIN ROBERTSON. ANDREW HUGHES. RICK FOLEY. PETER. LLOYD
FRONT ROW. NICK GEALE. JOHN WEBBER. NEIL AINSWORTH. JOHN CHEESEMAN. ERIC WILLIAMS. TROY BREEDEN

As well as playing Saturday mornings, we use to rush to the afternoon game vs the Men. Troy played in our Rep team and Rick played in both the School and Rep's team with me. All three of us played in the Saturday Senior team. Rick's Dad Mike, as well as our local Cricket Coach Bill, also played.

We actually Won the Comp with Troy (Boso) and myself hitting the winning runs. I still remember Mike filling up with tears as we both walked off. After the game, if we were playing close by it was back to Auburn RSL. Around that time I did a small Act calling the Greyhounds. I was given the microphone and use to call a dog race with everyone's name in it. All the cricketers loved cheering their dog on. Gealy's Pride seem to win every race and all the boys sung out "rigged", it was hilarious!

When we got old enough to drink, I think 15 years of age, we went on Tour. Boso's relatives lived in a small country town called Junee and the mini bus ride down was unreal. I got in trouble for being sick out the window and had to clean it up when we arrived. Boso's Dad Brian, loved Frank Senatra and sung "I did it my way". Fair Dinkum, you thought the roof of the bus was going to come off as everyone joined in the singing! I called a dog race and Gealy's Pride getting home by a nose! All the boys were cheering their dog on, it was complete Chaos!

On the Saturday morning we always played lawn bowls, hungover. It wasn't long and we'd be back on the drink. There was one memory I'll never forget. We stayed at a typical Country Pub with a balcony upstairs wrapping around the building. It was early evening and I decided to take my clothes off and slid down the timber supports. I ran naked away from the Pub and Boso was drinking a can of beer and launched it almost full from the balcony. The "Tooheys New" hit me bang smack on the back of my head, everyone cracked up! The Junee trips were a way to grow up quicker then most of the other kids our age. From memory we did three Tours?

GET AWAY:

A year after my Brother died, Mum and her best mate Margaret at #26 Charles Street decided to go away to Europe. I can only think it was my Mum's way to try as best as possible help her with the loss of her son. We were lucky that our neighbour June next door at #17 cooked us a meal. It was a weekly event and was the first time we ever ate hot chips! We always looked forward when it was her night to cook and Dad especially was exited as he had a night off.

Dad's specialty was Shepherds Pie. He didn't buy mince like every normal person. He'd cook a leg of lamb or beef the night before and put it through one of those old fashion mincers with a handle. He was always so pleased to present his cooked meal at the dinner table. It was a real challenge for Dad and Jim looking after 8 boys. I know they both were not happy with the length of the trip.

When Mum was away, Anthony was offered a glazing Apprenticeship. Even though he had not finished year 10, it was an opportunity worth considering. It was a Company literally around the corner at the bottom Shop named "On The Spot Glass". Back in the late 70s early 80s was a really good time to start a Business. It gave time for Businesses like "On The Spot" to really establish themselves. The Competition was a lot smaller and no interference with Online like now. Mum and Dad discussed the Apprenticeship on the phone and it was decided a good idea for Anthony to take it.

*Mum sent this when in Europe with Margaret, notice the
Name Assisi? St Francis is on my Brother's Memorial Card
handed out at his Funeral. I prayed for my Brother every night
for I can not remember, when I was growing up.*

Whilst Mum was in England she visited her Aunty in the North of
England. Her name too was Elsa and was the identical Twin to my
Grandmother, Mum's Mother. Back in the early 1900's they were both
to come to Australia and were only in their Teens. Elsa decided to stay
in England at the last moment. She watched her Sister board the ship
and they never met each other again! The ship sailed to Melbourne as
their Mother was already there. Can you imagine when their Mother
was waiting to see both her Daughters disembark the boat and only
one appeared?

After nearly 3 months away, Margaret and Mum returned back

from Europe. It was the start of many trips together. How fortunate two neighbours were able to forge such a great friendship! One of the reasons it was a life long relationship was from the early days they decided never to argue over the boys.

NEW SCHOOL:

Each year Mum went to the Parent Teacher nights and not forgetting she too was a Teacher! This was to be her last one at Oakhill College. My Brother Justin was very disruptive in the classroom and she decided that he moves. He was at the beginning of 4th form and he went to the State School, Muirfield High. It was located in North Rocks, on the same road I mentioned previously being constructed when I was in Primary School.

Report on .. *NICHOLAS... GEALE* ....

For period ending ...... *31-10-80* ....

Days absent .... *1* ....

General Comments

Nick has potential to do very well at school, but far too often he chooses to waste his time and, show off. I hope he settles down more next year.

K. Cox
....
Year Master

No. of subject reports: .... *9* ....

.... *RHM* ...... Principal

My Year 8 New School Report.

After his first day at the new School he met me at the bus stop near the fruit shop. He said, "your coming too"! Little did I know, it changed my life forever! We were not legally allowed to go there as we were on the wrong side of Windsor Road. This didn't stop Mum as she asked one of her good friends Margaret Parr, if it was ok to use their address? The answer was an instant Yes. I was always on edge if anyone wanted to see my Buss Pass as it had Ula Cres on it, not Charles Street!

It was there I met up again with my good mate from Primary and High School, Mark Pesavento, "Pes". He joined the School in Year 7 as it was called by then and I joined early in Year 8. My biggest change going to the new School was that we didn't have to wear a uniform. The other big change was there were also girls and it took me a while to adjust, however I knew Mum made the right decision.

Unfortunately I started hanging around some of the dodgy characters. They were into smoking Marijuana and although I tried it, luckily never took it up. I ended up drifting away from them and joined a tight group of mates, Pommy, Boh, Scotty, Marty and my old mate Pes! All of us were into Sport, so we had a connection that developed into life long friendships.

It was in Year 9 when I started asking myself what I wanted to do. Anthony as you know was a Glazier and Justin took up Plumbing. I decided I wanted to try Electrical. It was just before May of that Year and I grabbed Mum and Dad's Yellow Pages. I started to call Companies and asked if they had any Work Experience? I called Linden Electric and the Owner said "yes". Looking back now as a Father, can you imagine taking that call from a young kid?

I still vividly remember my first day. Kim, almost a Tradesman was sitting in the passenger seat, with me in the middle and Warren the Owner, driving. We arrived at a small building site and Kim jumped out of the van. He quickly slid the Toyota Hiace door open, grabbed a metal meter box, ran at least 20/30 yards, left it near a tree, ran back, jumped in the van and we took off quickly. I straight away knew what the pace was going to be.

Back to school. I knew if I wanted to get an Electrical Apprenticeship, I needed a Grade 1 in Maths. I knuckled down with Maths being my main subject and all the others were just fun! Talking about fun, our home room Teacher was also our Commerce Teacher. His name was Mr Young, Nic named Chuck. He was a scream and knew how to connect with us. There were times he'd walk into the classroom and we had reversed it totally around with his desk at the opposite end.

We hid the dusters used for the blackboard on the big steel supports for the ceiling. Chuck had a "lisp" and he'd ask, where are the "dusthters"? His famous saying when it was going off in class was, "Nick and your Mates, settle down"! We had a guy named Mark Homan who worked as a Volunteer Fireman. He'd stand up in Class, face the bush and ask all of us to follow suit, as he saluted the bush!

I unfortunately had a "flatulence" issue that later in life I was diagnosed Lactose Intolerant. Occasionally I'd let "go" in class and was sent out of the Classroom by Chuck. There'd be multiple times when the boys called out, "Gealy you stink" (when I did nothing) and was sent out of the Classroom! I sometimes wonder if Chuck ever reflected on our Class, this I will never know!

I was a target for some of the other kids as I was considered a "new comer" with a slightly bigger personality. I was on crutches after breaking my ankle on the cross country and a bloke in my Year was winding me up. I lost it and there I was having a "punch up" on one leg. It was split up and I was summoned to the Principal's Office. I was asked, "who was the other person in the fight"? I did not let on and it cost me a Black Mark. Nick Geale had arrived!

There was another bloke a year above me who bullied us younger kids. He was picking on a guy and I said to him "one day someone will sort you out"! The next I knew, there was a fight arranged at a Park on the way home the next day. I remember sitting on the back seat of the bus and asked Jeff Knight "what shall I do"? His reply was, "get the first punch in"!

I got off the bus on my own and walked to the Park, shitting myself! When I arrived, there was a big gathering at the other end of the Park. I kept walking straight through the crowd and whack, got the first punch in! It was an even contest. I remember lying on my bed later feeling my forehead as it had lumps all over it. I also had a cut below my lip where my tooth cut through and still have the scar today. My Parents never knew of the fight as we sorted stuff out on our own back then! The bloke I fought, never picked on me again!

At the back of #19. Uncle Mike is giving Anthony a kiss. Dad is wearing his Beirut as he always did, Justin far right.

MORE CRICKET:

As I have briefly mentioned, Cricket has been my passion and has shaped my Life as you read more. The last Selection Game for the Under 16 NSW Team was at Old Kings Oval just next door to Cumberland Oval, Parramatta. I made the Team and the first person I told was the fella who picked me up "Hitch Hiking" on Windsor Rd. The bloke worked out I played cricket as I had my whites on. I told him, "I have just made the NSW Team" and he asked, "what's your name son"? I replied, "Nick Geale" and he said, "I'll keep an eye out for you"!

The Carnival was to be played in Adelaide between Xmas and New Year. Late morning on Xmas Day 1981 Mum took a few photos at Charles Street before leaving to the Airport. It was my first time on a plane and I was anxious and still to this day I'd rather be on the ground than up there!

Christmas Day 1981 Before Leaving for the
Airport to Represent NSW Under16's.

I was carrying an injury with a sore knee and after a run early the next morning, I arrived back to my Hotel room in agony. I never let on as I didn't want to miss out on the Tournament. I was not the only Wicket Keeper in the team as it was shared with Andrew Milican (Spike) who went on to play for Randwick and had a great Career.

My memories are vague, although I do remember stumping a guy vs Victoria, his name was Gerard Clarke. It was not until a good 10 years later after Rick moved to Melbourne he became good mates with Gerard. To this day "Clackers" as he is called, reckons he was not out, don't you love the "Banta" in Sport!

At the end of the Carnival our Manager Graham Erington came to my room. He said, "if you played all the games, You'd be in the Australian Team as Keeper"! The player who got the Australian job ended up playing Sheffield Shield cricket for Tasmania. He "kept" in all the games and totalled 25 points and I missed I think 2 games and I was on 23 points!

I was playing 4th Grade for my first Grade Club Balmain, at the time. As I was too young to drive, once again Dad came to the rescue. We picked up Boso at his home in Ermington and we drove the back roads to Drummoyne Oval. Dad and Boso always talked about the Greyhounds and after dropping us off he went to Drummoyne RSL and played the Pokies. Boso and I still talk about those days in the Datsun with Dad! I made my way to 3rd Grade, however in front of me were two guys in their 20's and both good Keepers. More on this later.

Booklet for Carnival

NSW Team.Year 1981

NSW Under 16 Year 81/82. Robbo is far right
back row, Foles is 2 in from him. Me?

LEAVING SCHOOL:

I got my Grade 1 in Maths and I still joke, I was the first out the gate from School when the year was over. We all went away up to Forster to celebrate the end of Year 10. Pommy drove and it was early on in the trip I brought up how "tight" he was! All of us were getting the "shits" with it and someone needed to air it. His Dad being Welsh, who are renown for being careful with their money was rubbing off on him. I said, "all of us are getting pissed off with you not buying your round of drinks, when it's your turn"! We all still laugh about it as he was not aware of it and never was a problem again. We arrived in Forster and camped in one of the Caravan Parks. Boh made a classic remark that till this day we take the piss out of him. He was a big fisherman and he said, "we will eat off the land"! From memory there was no fish on the BBQ, just snags and cheap steaks.

If anyone has been to Forster they know the Bridge separating Forster and Tuncurry. It is a good couple of hundred metres and Pommy and I decided to swim it. When we arrived at one end, luckily there was a guy Hiring flippers. We both whacked them on and off we went with the guy quite concerned. What we didn't take into account was there was a possibility Sharks may be around as it was the entrance to the Ocean. We survived and both have a laugh all these years later!

Forster after leaving Year 10. Boh, Pom, Pes and me.Year 1982.

I officially started my Electrical Apprenticeship in January 1983. I was so lucky that Dad drove me to Kellyville for Six months. I went to Blacktown Tech once a week and worked the other 4 days. As I mentioned earlier, luckily I knew what was expected. My Apprenticeship was the toughest going. Warren was a "hard" task Master and so too was Kim.

Once we arrived on Site it was straight into it! There was no standing around and I unloaded the tools needed for the day. I was always taught to think ahead and if I wasn't on the ball, I knew about it Immediately! If it was a new house, Kim was literally "running" from spot to spot drilling, wiring and hammering away. I too copied him, it was fast going!

I longed for "Smoko", just to have a break. This was where I got the nic name "Havachat"! All I wanted to do was talk, when Kim especially just wanted to have a small nap. Warren on the other hand was always interested in talking. He was a perfectionist, starting with an official uniform and we wore name badges. The vans were sign written like no other Company, bright, bold, hard to miss. He was also into

Technology and always wanting an edge on his Competitors. We had a two way radio form of communication in those early days. It was not long before he invested in a Mobile Phone. I still remember him carrying a large battery which was attached to the phone unit.

My Work Van, Warren loved the Bright Signage and Technology, Radio Controlled.

It was my job to make sure all the tools were back in the van at the end of each day. Once I left a thin gas bottle used to solder the earth cables on Site. Warren deducted the amount for a new one out of my wages. I am not sure how many Bosses have done that but it taught me a lesson and I never lost another tool after that!

I had long wild hair in those days and as I was drilling on top of a ladder, my hair got caught in the drill. Luckily I was working with Kim so he helped me down. The drill ripped some hair out of my scalp and Kim had to tell Warren I needed to go to the Doctors. Warren wasn't happy and I felt he was more concerned about the time lost rather then my well being.

There was another time when I was at Cricket training at Bankstown Oval. My work van was parked in the School next door. Dean Waugh hit the ball over the fence and smashed the side mirror. I told Warren who naturally was not happy and I was made to pay for a new one!

Sometimes being too honest can be a setback! Although he was hard, he was fair and later on you will understand this.

Role on nearly 30 years and Linden Electric Celebrated 40 Years in Service. I went along for Respect to Warren and the Sacrifices he made through my Apprenticeship. I was Apprentice #3 and got up to Speak. I took the Piss out of Warren's funny Questions! "Have I Showered this morning"? "Where is your Name Badge"? "What's the Capital of Brussels"?

When he was in a good mood, he'd sing "Roll out the Barrow", "We'll have a Barrow of Fun". I started to sing the Song and went over to his Table and we both sung it and the rest of the Guests joined in. It was a Great Night and he has Officially passed the Batten across to his Son James, who is a really nice young Man.

MATESHIP:

July 1985, Pommy and I were turning 19 and we organised a Party at #19 at late notice. We were not really sure how many may turn up. Our smallish backyard was full and the back room had the TV on with the "Live Aid" Concert in London. It was great dancing and we partied all night. How lucky were we to coincide our Milestone with such a Global Event!

Pommy and I Celebrating our 19th Birthday's, amazing night!
Boh is in Blue and Davy Williams is wearing the Hat!

May 1986, Pes, Pommy, Marty and myself went on a Cruise on the famous Fairstar through the Pacific Islands. Boh didn't come and I know deep down is one of his life regrets. When we were standing on the deck waving goodbye to all the families below there were a few blokes standing near us and for some reason we all connected. From leaving Sydney and arriving back 14 days later, is was partying, sleeping, partying and more sleeping.

Our Ship Fairstar, how good are the shorts!

Cruise May 1986, Pom, Pes, Me and Marty. Sadly, Marty passed away just 6 months later from a Motor Bike accident.

CRICKET:

I needed to leave Balmain and looked around all the other Clubs and I decided on Bankstown. The main reason was, the Keeper in 1st Grade was in his early 30's, his name was Les Andrews. I was graded in the 3rd team and went to 2nd's quite quickly and met a guy who was to be a life long friend, Geoff Spotswood. He was Captain and taught me how to play hard cricket. He also played 1st grade Rugby League and his work ethic especially with training rubbed off on me. I was in the 2nd's for a season and a half learning my trade.

My great mate Spotty and his wife Barb.

I knew I was close in getting promoted to the 1st Team as I was happy with my Keeping. Spotty my 2nd Grade Captain came via 19 Charles on the way home from Selection night. He knocked on the door and had a general chit chat. I was hoping he was going to say, I was selected but he never brought it up. He left and about 5 minutes later, he knocked on the door again giving me the good news.

I am Keeping and the bowler is David Freedman who went on to play Sheffield Shield for NSW. Season 1984/85 2nd Grade, vs St George

The rest is a blur and I played my first game in 1st Grade aged 19. In the team were a few State and Australian players, Steve Smith (not the current one playing now) Steve and Mark Waugh, David Freedman, Rod Bower and Wayne Holdsworth .

One day playing at North Sydney Oval after fielding on a hot day we went for lunch. I was on the toilet and Timmy Sullivan was mucking around and threw some "cold water" over the door. I jumped up and pushed my hand on the door to open and chase him. Unfortunately my hand went straight through the glass on the door and cut my wrist. Little did I know this incident had long term ramifications to my career!

I went to Royal North Shore Hospital with Wayne Holdsworth's Father Larry. After examining they wanted to simply stitch me up. I told them how important my hands were as a Wicket Keeper and Electrician and they decided to get some scans done. Thank God they did as my tendon was severed 75%. I had surgery that night and the magnitude set in. It was late January, early February and I had organised a Season in England to play in the Kent League with my mate Neil Jones, Pommy.

ENGLAND:

Pommy and Me heading to the UK to play Cricket!

It was early April 1987 when Pommy and I set off to play Cricket for Folkestone Cricket Club. When I left Baulkham Hills, the last thing my Mother said to me was, "don't come back with an English Bride". More on that later. We paid for the cheapest fare with Garuda Air. It stopped 6 or 7 times before reaching Gatwick in the South of England. My first recollection as we caught a bus for London was, where were all the houses? There were green fields full of cattle and farm houses and it looked so vast. Eventually we hit London and all the congestion started.

We caught our next bus to the Midlands of England where Pommy's relatives lived. I worked out that from the time I left Baulkham Hills and arrived at Stourport-on-Severn, it took 72 hours. It was the first time I have ever experienced Jet-lag and it took a few days to get back to normal. Hearing the English accent on their home soil was also a bit strange. After staying there a few days, Pommy and I left for London as I was going on a Contiki Tour through Europe.

So here I am, on my own ready to take on a Trip of a life time. We all met up in London's Russell Square. When we got on the bus, I headed straight for the back. Just like the school bus, all the good blokes hung out there and I was spot on! Scott our Tour Guide introduced himself and let us all know about our "Theme Song" to be played each morning when on the bus. It was "All I need is a Miracle" by Mike and the Mechanics.

We headed for Dover to catch the Ferry for France. It was just after the Ferry Disaster that sunk, killing hundreds of people. I still remember boarding the Ferry and noticed the big doors where all the cars were to drive in. Apparently the doors were not closed correctly and water rushed in, causing the boat to sink.

We spent the next 21 days travelling through France, Germany, Italy, Austria and Holland. My job was to pack the bags on the bus, ready to go to our next destination. I was always late, mainly hungover. I never let them down at the other end when we arrived. My doctor suggested that I use a squeeze ball to help me with my recent surgery on my wrist. There was plenty of time on the bus to use it, with holding onto a can of beer in the other!

In Rome we went into the Vatican. As young Niave Aussie's, we thought it was too busy and we went to the Pub instead! I did take in St Peter's Square and was amazed how all the columns were so straight and how they all lined up at any angle. We also went shopping in Italy for mainly leather. I bought a leather jacket as they are famous for them. Unfortunately that jacket is no longer in my wardrobe! Why are we not allowed to keep things that mean a lot to us? Answer, being married!

From Italy it was off to Germany and we all went to one of those German traditional drinking places. The Waitresses carried at least 4 Steiner glasses on each hand and it was chaos! The next day to sober up we went for a swim in Munich's Olympic Pool. After showering, I noticed a wallet on the ground and I asked if it was one of ours? It was full of German currency and we worked it out to be approximately $600 Australian dollars. We split it three ways with Pete and his girl. We partied heavily that night using the found prize and it also came in handy to pay the beer bill that I accumulated on the bus!

*Contiki Tour in Amsterdam. I am towards
the top in middle. Year 1987.*

Austria was our next location and we stayed in a small Hotel with another Contiki Tour party. We were sadly informed of an accident with one of their group who was killed crossing a road in Spain. It's one of those moments that stick with you and looking back now, when the news reached home must have been devastating to the family! Their theme song was "Another one bites the Dust", it was changed immediately!

Holland was our final stop and one of the boys was always talking about going to one of the Brothels when in Amsterdam. True to his word, he walked up the stairs and a good 15 minutes later, open the doors with a massive smile on his face. All of us cheered him from across the road!

After 21 days we headed back to England on a ferry. I left the tour party on the Port as the rest headed back to London. It was sad saying goodbye as we all got on so well.

FOLKESTONE CRICKET CLUB:

Folkestone was a good two to three hours from the Port. I bought a one way ticket and caught at least three trains until finally arriving at Folkestone. I still remember jumping in a Black Cab and contemplating about my next four months. It was early Evening and I arrived at 209 Cheriton Rd in only 5 minutes. After paying for the Cab, I looked up at the row of tall houses all joined together and thought, this is my home for the next 4 to 5 months!

I walked up the front stairs and knocked on the door. It seemed to take ages, so I looked through the small flap where the mail is put through. Slowly, this little old lady was walking down the stairs. She opened the door and I said hello, "I'm Nick" and gave her a kiss. Her name was Mrs Dawson who was known as Mrs D.

I took my bag up three flights of stairs to our bedroom which was in the Attic. Pommy had arrived earlier with my Cricket Kit in the corner and I asked Mrs D where he was? She said, "down the Cricket Club" and gave me directions. I headed to the Club which was only a few minutes away. I walked up the stairs of the old Pavilion and noticed some barn style doors were closed. With my adrenaline flowing, I opened the doors and said G'Day!

I had my new leather jacket on that I bought in Italy and everyone looked at me. They were just finishing up on a meeting and I spotted Pommy. I walked straight over to him and it settled me down a bit. This is what we both came over for and from that moment I was taken on unbelievably well.

We met some characters that night and one guy stood out. When introducing himself, he said "hi, my name is David and I have a Twin Brother". His Brother was just folk lore, he was such a funny bloke and when on the beers DC was hilarious! There was another bloke in his mid to late 30's, Roy Downey. Little did I know he was to become a life long friend, more later.

The very next day, Pommy and I went down to the Ground. I wanted to see how my hand was going to cope. I started catching tennis balls and soon was catching cricket balls. After a good session it felt ok, what a relief!

Folkestone was a Kent County Ground and Don Bradman played there back in the 30's. It had a massive square with at least 20 pitches across it. At one end was the old Pavilion and the other was open to the elements. On top of the hills beyond, there were the words "NO TUNNEL" made with rocks.

Folkestone Cricket Club 1987

*Pommy and I at Folkestone CC, He is wearing his Parramatta Cap
and I am wearing my Bankstown Cap. Late April/May Year 1987.*

Kent is a big County and it sometimes took over an hour to arrive at some of the grounds. It was always worth the journey as mainly all picturesque. There was a Motor Way that connected everything and boy do they drive quickly over there.

Quite early after we arrived, both Pommy and I looked for a job. We both got one at Folkestone Pizza Hut. It was great fun earning money to pay for mainly beers and a few trips here and there. We actually made the paper wearing our uniform and looking back now how funny is that!

There was an interesting shift at the Pizza Hut one night. Just after closing time for the Pubs a group of young people came in. They ordered their Pizza and for some reason the order was stuffed up and put back in the queue. When the 2nd Pizza arrived, the young bloke who was pissed said, "I'm not paying for this"! I whispered in his ear, "not only are you going to pay for it, your going to Fucking eat it"!

Pommy and I at Pizza Hut Folkestone.

I walked away and his Pizza was slung across the restaurant. He barged past our Manageress and before you knew it, I was having a punch up with him outside, near the entrance. Pommy came over to break it up! A few weeks after that, Pommy and I were in the kitchen waiting for the Pizzas to come out of the revolving oven. "Smash", a half brick was thrown through a back window and scared the shit out of us! It literally bounced directly on the area where we sliced the Pizzas up. We both immediately thought, a revenge attack!

We travelled to London regularly if we had a few days off. We caught up with my mate Rick who was playing near Newcastle up North. We had a laugh one day at Madame Tussaud's. I was standing really "still" near a wall and some visitors came past and said, "who's that?" I jumped and scared them big time, both Rick and I were in hysterics.

On another trip to London I visited the iconic Lillywhites Sports Store in Piccadilly. I caught the lift to the Cricket section and noticed a lot of activity. I realised it was one of my idles growing up, Viv Richards. He was signing autographs and I put one leg over a small chain. The lady said, "sorry he has finished" and I replied, "I've travelled all the way from Australia for this"! She said, "ok" and before I knew it, I was shaking hands with Viv! Meeting someone with his profile was a bit surreal and the poster he signed is now framed in my Cricket Room.

Meeting Viv Richards, Lillywhites London.

About half way through the Season, I heard bad news back home regarding my Cricket. Bankstown had appointed an Ex County player to Captain their 1st Grade Team. Unfortunately, he was also a Keeper so I was not required. I still have the original letter dated 1st July 1987.

It was a hard time trying to comprehend their decision and being so far away added to the situation. I know there were a few of my team mates especially Spotty who stuck up for me. Looking back now, I understood their decision, although I didn't agree to it but unfortunately being a "Keeper" there is only one in any team.

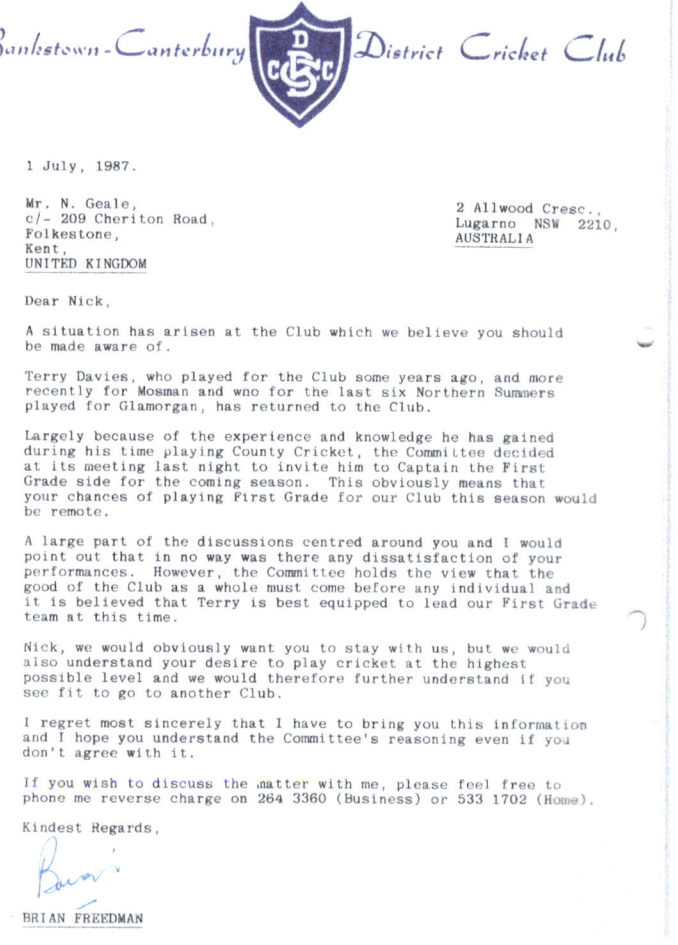

Letter from Bankstown CC letting me go!

It was now July and Folkestone's Tour was in Worcester. I remember driving up North and it was the first time I spotted Concord. Remember, I was a young kid from Sydney and seeing Concord Live was amazing. When we arrived Rick who somehow "conned" his way on to the Tour was playing pool with the locals. The Pub was called The Great Western, bang smack in the middle of Worcester.

*Tour to Worcester, DC is in the Check shirt and
Roy is Facing down, note the Date!*

Unfortunately the weather was not great and we had a few games
called off. There was an old bloke who joined us most evenings, he
said he was a Doctor. David Curran, DC took an instant liking towards
him and were two peas in a pod. Doc as we called him, took out his
false teeth and slept on the bar benches. There were also some other
locals who worked at the main Post Office on shift work. They'd turn
up at 4/5 in the morning and start drinking and jotted down the drinks
and paid it at a later date.

Pommy and I were lucky to have our 21st Birthday mid week. They
organised a cake for us and we all had a great night. We both really
struggled the next day and unfortunately the weather improved and
had to play. I still remember Pommy lying on the grass with a huge
hangover as we were batting.

Our last game was at Kidderminster, another County Ground. We
all played and some of the Folkestone boys were in the other Team.
Roy was keen to Open the Batting and faced Pommy steaming in. He
nicked one and it flew to Gary Wadups in Slip who took a good catch.
Roy walked off and we all met in the middle of the pitch celebrating
the moment. It was at that time Gary made a comment, "That was like

a Test Match"! It was not only the words but his dry English accent has stuck with me and Pommy forever.

Remember when I mentioned previously about my Mother's Aunty? The boys headed back to Folkestone and I caught a train South and got off at Thirsk. Next was a bus to near a small little village named Kirbymoorside in Yorkshire. I remember walking along a Country road with only a few cows in the paddocks. Travelling by yourself is sometimes so surreal, it was so peaceful. I entered the Village and went to the local Butchers asking, "do they know a lady called Elsa Maw"? The fella said, "yes she lives in a small cottage just down the road".

Just picture the situation, those blokes working in the Butcher Shop and this young Aussie walks in. I wonder how many Aussie tourists have ever been through that Shop? Ok, I set off and as I was heading towards the small cottage, I looked down a lane way and spotted this little old lady walking directly towards me. It was my Great Aunt (or my Grandmother, her twin Sister) walking towards me. As she and her little dog got closer to me, I said "Hi, I'm Elsa's son Nicholas". She was a bit puzzled but remembered I was in England as Mum wrote to her.

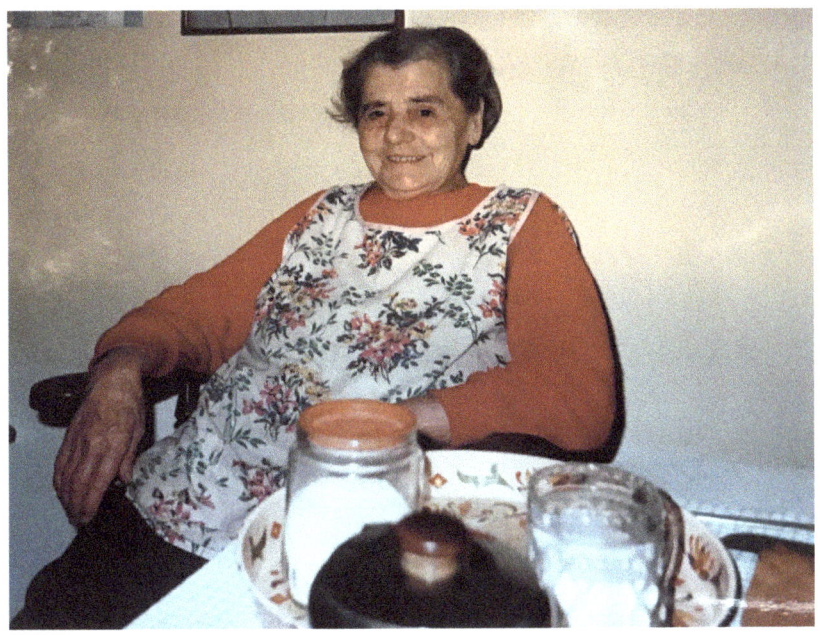

My Great Aunty Elsa in her little home.
Go back to page 21 to see the comparisons of her Sister taken at a similar age.

We went back to her little place for a cup of tea and she had the same idiosyncrasies as my Grandmother. Aunty Elsa asked me "how is Doris going"? I had to cover up my answer and said, "she is ok". Unfortunately my Grandmother had early Dementia but I did not think I'd achieve anything by letting on. We went out to the garden and took a photo with the automatic timer and she was amazed by the technology.

I arrived back at Folkestone and we played Cricket, worked and kept enjoying ourselves. A few weeks later Rick came down for a visit and he and Pommy went up to the shops and booked a holiday to Corfu. Back in those days there was a gap in the Season, so the timing was perfect. To be honest, I was not that keen to go, I was out voted, so Greece here we come!

It was mid August 1987 and we arrived in Corfu. We caught the bus and it stopped at lots of Hotels and we were saying, "that looks good". We were one of the last to be dropped off and we arrived at a "dingy" looking place. I said, "what the Fuck is this joint"? No doubt Rick

(Foles) and Pommy picked the cheapest Hotel in the book! I remember walking around next morning thinking we have been stitched up!

Drinks at the Boomerang Bar with Pom and Foles.

The only thing going for it was the local bar was called the Boomerang Bar. I always wondered why was it called that in Corfu, fair enough Bali, where all the Aussie's went but Corfu? There were lots of activities to choose and we decided to pick "Mud Wrestling" as we thought "Chicks" may come along. We wore straw hats and tied corks on them as well as zinc cream on our noses, looking like real Aussies! We caught the bus and headed towards the back passing three girls. Naturally they noticed three "Spunks" walking past them. As we sat down, we spoke about them and happy that we made our Tour selection!

We arrived at the Beach and we played this game with a cucumber. I was paired up with a blonde chick and straight after bought her a drink. I asked her what was her name, she replied "Amanda"! Next was a classic drinking race. You had to skull a drink, run in a few circles and try find your way back to where we started. As you can imagine, everyone was running away from the target, it was hilarious!

Next was the main event, Mud Wrestling. There were six blokes and six chicks. The three girls on the bus, one being Amanda and us three guys volunteered. The chicks had to pick their Partner and I was chosen 2nd last with Foles being last! It was the same chick I bought a drink for previously, Amanda. I had to put one arm behind my back and it was wrestle time. You've never witnessed a scene like it, mud everywhere, it was brilliant. At the end we had a group photo. Amanda was sitting in between my legs, both facing the audience. As soon as "say cheers" was called, I pulled down her swimming top and her little white "tits" were facing everyone! The whole crowd were in hysterics!

*I'm cuddling Amanda, Poms next to me
and Foles is at the back, no mud!*

Jane, Me and Amanda on my left in Corfu.

We hung out together, either at the pool or the Boomerang Bar. It was around the time Johnny Farnham brought out "Down the barrel of a Gun". When the Song came on it was electric and we took over the Joint. One night there was a girl walking around selling Roses. I bought one and rather then romantically walking over to Amanda, I decided to throw it over to her and she caught it.

Amanda left earlier then us and we all went to a place called

Paliacastritssa on the island. It's one of those places that even now I still remember, let alone pronounce it!

We soon arrived back in England and I went straight to her town called Reading. It is located along the M4 Motorway heading west from London. You pass Windsor Castle which I have a bit to say about later. Amanda rented a room in a little flat and I stayed there a few days.

We finished playing cricket in early September and had a great send off! Our time at Folkestone was over and an experience of a lifetime that I will never forget! Saying goodbye to Mrs Dawson (Mrs D) and Ian was emotional. It was their home that we enjoyed for just over four months and as young blokes we really appreciated the sacrifices they made.

Pommy, Ian ,Mrs D and Myself saying "Goodbye"!

ENGLAND KENT LEAGUE

GEALY AND POMMY

Our "Last" night at Folkestone CC. When I look back it gives me
"Fantastic" feelings. I was blessed to go to such a Great Club with such
Top Blokes and spend it with Pommy was Unmatchable! Roy is at the
very back, Great Mate. I still have my "Tankard" in my Cricket Room.

We jumped into the cab with shit loads of luggage. We headed to Ashford to get money out of the ATM. We were "skint" and our cards did not work! The cabbie said, "no problem, send me the money when you get back home". We were so taken back by the offer and he drove us to Gatwick Airport. As soon as we arrived home, the money was sent to the cab driver! Amanda came to the Airport to say goodbye. Although it was decided she'd travel to Australia the following year, it still was very, very sad!

On our way home we stopped off at Bali to unwind and get ready for the Season ahead. We stayed a week and when I was near the entrance at Denpasar Airport I thought best I discard my "flick" knife I bought in Italy. Although it was in my large kit and not hand luggage, I had a feeling it may be found and who knows what may have come from that?

BACK HOME:

When I arrived home at #19, Mum organised a large sign and hung it out the front garden saying "Nick, We have missed You!" She is so much like me and loves people feeling good about themselves. Let me tell you, when I saw the sign I felt a million bucks and I gave Mum a big hug! I went straight around to see Pes and it was good to see him again.

Pommy and I went to our new club, Campbeltown. We thought if we can play at the same Club, we'd share the cost of travel as it was a good 45mins away. It was agreed that Pommy play 1st Grade and I play 2nd Grade with the one condition, I was given the opportunity to go up if the situation arose. It wasn't long and the 1st team keeper was dropped, so I naturally thought I'm in. They decided to play a batsman in 1st's, who kept wicket a bit. They totally went back on the Agreement and was clear that I was not really wanted and the hidden Agenda was to get Pommy to the Club!

Outside #19 after 6 Months away. Sign done
by Mum. I'm 21 & Mum 50.

When I heard the news at training, I was fuming. I walked over to the Captain of 1st Grade (who was part of the deal) with my kit and being a straight shooter, told him exactly what I thought of him! I jumped in my car and never played for them again. It was a "Sliding Doors" moment and looking back now, how things may have changed if I was selected in 1st Grade? As it turned out, Pommy got stress fractures in his back and they lost out in the end! Due to the timing, it was too late trying to join another Grade Club that season, so I went back to Pennant Hills to keep my skills up. Yet again, another set back!

Towards the end of 1987 I had my belated 21st Birthday. It was at Charles Street and it was great to see friends that I had not seen for a good 9 months. The next morning after waking, I noticed my car was not out the front. We walked around the streets and found it just around the corner, all smashed up. It was a really awkward situation as we knew who the culprit was but did not want to start a rift. I only heard recently from Mum that she wrote down the events of that night and pinned it in her wardrobe. At the end of the day, that person has to live with the fact he crashed my car!

AMANDA ARRIVES:

It was early 1988 and I picked up Amanda from Sydney Airport. She was coming over to Australia to see me and travel with her two friends, Jane and Jo. I took her to Sydney Harbour and we have a great photo with the iconic Harbour Bridge in the background. She fitted into the family and forged a close relationship with my Mum.

Amanda and I went on a holiday to New Zealand and travelled mainly around the South Island. When we were in Wellington I caught up with Simon who worked at Linden Electric. He showed both of us around and it was great to catch up with him. Unfortunately I have lost contact over the years, a great guy Simon! I also was lucky to watch a days play in a Cricket Test Match, NZ vs England at Basin Reserve.

Our highlite was flying over Frans Joseph Glazier and landing on it too. Not sure if we'd do the same thing today, now that we are both Parents? We headed to Milford Sound and when on the water you understood why it is such a great draw card for anyone visiting the South Island. We hired a small car and stayed at B&B's which was an easy way to get around. New Zealand is such a unique country and we really enjoyed our time there.

Amanda and the Girls left to tour around Australia, it was about

March, April. I was working as a Sparky for a new company, PM Cork. I was like a lost lamb whilst she was away. The only way of communication was an expensive phone box call or by letters.

There was a funny moment when I called a Hostel in Nth Queensland. Someone answered the phone and I asked if Amanda was there? The reply was "no she's at Jeff's Place". I said, "who the "Fuck" is Jeff", thinking the worst? Jeff's Place happens to be another small Hostel to stay and we still laugh about it to this day!

Finally, she got back to Sydney and soon after we went to Hawaii. It was a great trip and we caught up with Aunty Elaine and the kids on their way back from America. Uncle Mick never went, his excuse was to stay home and work to pay for the trip. He is just a home bod, also does not like flying.

Amanda and I just after she arrived from England.

It was not long after getting back and Amanda answered a phone call at home and wrote down the details. When I got home from work she said, "a guy called Trevor Chappell called asking for you". She had no idea who he was and I called him back straight away. We met up with the President and they asked me if I'd be interested in playing at North Sydney. It was only a 2nd Grade spot but I thought why not and played one season for them, finishing in the Semifinals. All the blokes in the team had a great sense of humour with lots of slang, banter etc. I had such a laugh with them.

One night in Epping I bumped into Terry McMahon who played for Balmain. He made a smart arse comment about me playing at several clubs. I had to remind him that in a team there is only one keeper and if you want to play at a high level, getting a start can be more difficult than a bowler or batsman. He got the message, no angst, I just stood my ground!

Amanda left home for the UK early 1989 having spent a year in Australia. I decided to follow her back a bit later. Mum was always thinking ahead and said to me, "you need to buy a block of land"! It was as a backup and a good way to save my money whilst away. I bought a block in Umina, from memory around 30/35 thousand dollars. It was a steep block, hence the cheaper price compared to a nice flat one.

We had a good piss up with the boys in the City before leaving. We went to the Pump House Pub near the old Entertainment Centre. After consuming lots of beers we went to the Shooting Ducks side show nearby. All the prizes were gathered at the bottom and as I held the slug gun, I whispered to Steve Pes, "watch this". Rather than trying to shoot at the ducks in a line, I aimed straight at a plastic cup half full of orange juice. I didn't miss and the drink went all over the prizes. We bolted and the store owner started to chase but gave up. It was good to get all the boys together and a few weeks later I was off to England.

LEAVING HOME:

Going to England this time was different. I wasn't going for my love of cricket. I was going for a different love! Amanda picked me up at the airport and we headed back to her home in Reading. It was the first time I met her Parent's, Keith and Margaret. Keith was a Policeman and from day one I showed the utmost respect for him.

Amanda's Brother Simon lived downstairs with her Parents and we stayed upstairs. After settling in I hunted for a job. I got a start at a Sport Shop in Reading Town Centre. I also went to my first training session with Reading Cricket Club. Before I left Australia I wrote to them letting them know I was a Keeper, Batsman. They came back saying, the 1st Team Keeper was in the Minor Counties Berkshire Team and therefore meant I was to play in the 2nd's. When I arrived at the nets, I was informed the 2nd team Captain was also a Keeper! I was disappointed but I didn't let it rattle me and I just accepted it.

I missed the first trial game because we went to Folkestone for the weekend. When we got back I was graded in the 4th's and I was shattered! I backed my own ability and said to myself, knuckle down and show them what I am capable off. It wasn't long and I was playing 3rd Grade and made 97 Not Out.

The Captain was a guy called Ian McDougall, Mac. Little did I know we'd be friends to this day! Mac is about 10 years older then me but we just clicked from day one. I made the 2nd team as a batsman and not Keeping was unusual to me. On the Sundays I played in the 1st team and kept wicket to keep my skills up.

Amanda worked with a girl called Caroline and made a great friendship as well as Tim her Husband. Amanda and Caroline were both anxious if their other halves clicked. I remember going to their house for the first time with Amanda. I shook Tim's hand and he offered me a beer and straight away we got on well. It was better than the girls may have hoped for. He too was a Sparky and played Rugby and also has a great sense of humour.

After working at the Sports Shop for about 4 months, Tim asked me if I'd like to get back on the tools? I said no worries and we travelled to Watford which is a good hour plus trip from Reading. I'd be about the third person to be picked up just down the road from Amanda's Parents and next was Nick Barnes. At least once a week he slept in and looked out the window saying "two minutes" and raced to the van and off we'd go. The foreman was Frank and he too travelled with us. He was a small miserable little prick. He came from Liverpool and was as tight as a fish's arse!

On site it was a real laugh. I'd work with Tim and you always had to be on your guard. I went to the "dunny" one day and after returning, I'd tried to lift my tool box off the scaffold. It was screwed to the wooden base and I nearly tore my shoulder socket out when attempting to lift it, great fun. Smoko was always good fun, however I noticed often they'd talk about how much they were being paid. This was strange to me as back home money was never discussed. We all got on well, with all the boys calling me OZ.

Amanda and I in Barbados. Year 1989.

Late Dec 1989 Amanda and I went on a Tour to Barbados with Folkestone CC. We played at least three games and the way they hit the ball is something I have never experienced. They are so carefree and when they hit a Six into the houses the batsman casually turns to the Clubhouse and requests another ball. I can honestly say we lost about 6/8 balls that day!

All the boys with Jansen our Bus Driver.

There were lots of funny moments but this really explains why the West Indians are so laid back. We got picked up one day in a small mini bus. We all piled in with our gear and it was hot as! Jansen was our driver for the whole Tour and he started driving out the Hotel roundabout heading along the driveway. About half way he stops the Mini Bus, opens his door, gets out and with his hanky he wipes the sweat away from his forehead. He jumps back in and starts driving away with all of us sweating in the back!

Just before the Toss, I am seeing how hard the Pitch is
with keys; notice how close the houses are.

Catching the Bus to the Town of Barbados was an unbelievable experience. The music was blasting with Reggae and some of the locals dancing in the isle. Once we arrived it was so interesting watching the locals. The girls went and got their hair braided and we went to some of the local bars.

I really want to go back to the West Indies one day to watch a Test Series. The great thing is, Amanda is interested in Cricket too, so let's hope so?

BACK TO UK:

I lasted till Xmas as a Sparky and read a job advert in the paper for an Electrical Wholesaler Rep. I was always interested in Sales and I thought why not give it a go. I never owned a suit so I borrowed one from a guy at the Cricket Club. I was lucky to get the job because the original guy pulled out, another "Sliding Doors" moment. The Manager of the Wholesaler who gave me a start was Juan Ruiz. Little did I know he became a very close Friend and Mentor.

On my 2nd day he asked me to go and see what's happening at a Town about 30 miles along the M4 Motorway, called Swindon. I went to heaps of Building Sites giving out my card and really enjoyed it. A few days later, the Swindon Manager called Juan, asking "why was I down in his territory?" I obviously made an impression and I said to Juan, "you asked me to look around, so I did exactly that". We laugh about it to this day!

Back to Mac, he also loved Rugby and in that first Winter was the Lions Tour to Australia. When the games were on, for a bit of exercise I rode on a bike to his house early morning in the freezing cold. We still talk about that "pass" from David Campese in his own try area. He was always so unpredictable and stuffed up with the Lions scoring. After Xmas 1990, Mac got a new job in Leeds and asked Amanda and I if we'd like to house sit their home? It was good timing as we got the chance to live with each other on our own.

We stayed in Mac's house and not long after I was approached by a local club Boyne Hill to come and play for them. I travelled up the old A4 to go and have a chat with them. When I walked into the Clubhouse, a fella came out of the dressing rooms carrying a paint brush. He introduced himself as Rod Mills, the President. I straight away felt comfortable that if the President is prepared to get stuck in, then it's the Club for me.

There was also another bloke who I met at the stairs looking out to the main ground. I said G'day and asked what team he played in and his reply was "keep wicket" in the 1st". Although it was a little uncomfortable, it was good to settle the keeping situation early. His name was Steve Palfrey (Palfs) and we became good friends.

The same week I went to meet Boso at Heathrow Airport. He was to play in England and as soon as we got in the car he started to talk about this girl back in Sydney. I said, "mate pull your head in, you have a great opportunity over here"! He didn't listen to me and was back home in a few weeks.

The weekend after, I played on the Sunday as the Saturday was a National Knockout Competition and Oversees players were not allowed to play; from memory it was a two year rule. We played at Bracknell on the Sunday, the same town Amanda worked at the Saloon. I got there early and met a fella in the dressing rooms. He introduced himself as Patrick and I joked with him asking if he got a bit of "sex" last night? He laughed and I said, "I did and means you generally get runs"! Guess what, I scored a Hundred in my very first innings for the Club, my theory worked!

The following weekend was the start of the League. We were away to Amersham, a nice typical English ground. We won the toss and bowled first as all the games were One Dayers and the best way to get a result. A fella came in the middle order who was their Overseas Player and scored a few quick runs. When we got back in the dressing rooms Paul King our Captain called out the batting line up. To my surprise, I was number 3 and took off my keeping gear and started to get my mindset onto batting.

The Clubhouses over there are all so unique. I've always enjoyed looking at all the old photos. Cricket has so much History and it was in England my interest started reading about the Game and collecting things on the way.

I walked around the Clubhouse at tea feeling a bit nervous. I read an article on the notice board about their Oversees Player, Damien Fleming. He was over on a Scholarship and was a highly respected fast bowler from Melbourne. He later went on to play Test and One Day games for Australia. He bowled the last over in the Semi Final vs South Africa in the 1999 World Cup. South Africa had the momentum but a mix up with Lance Kluesner and Allan Donald ending in a runout, with Australia going on to Win the Tournament!

We were chasing from memory no more than 150 and I was lucky to be not out scoring 50. I still recall pulling Fleming for a four to win the game! It was the start to a Season that Boyne Hill CC have never witnessed, more on that later.

In about the June of 1990, Juan left the Company we worked at and joined a Competitor called Edmundsons in the Town Slough. Amanda and I had just moved into our new Home at the same time. It was on the outskirts of Reading, bordering a Town called Caversham. When Juan left he contacted me to come and work for him. I wasn't sure what to do as I had only been working as a Sales Rep for less than 6 months. I asked a Customer his thoughts and Harry said, "if it's more money why not"! I decided to go, however my Manager came around to visit me to try and change my mind. It was a bit further away but I went with my gut feel and another decision that was to shape my career.

Outside Amanda's Parents home with my Company Car; how good is the Suit!

NEW JOB:

I was the Rep for the outskirts of Slough and the previous Manager looked after inner Slough. My job was to hunt new business as well as looking after existing customers. Juan employed a guy who he knew in the same industry as Assistant Manager. Sean was totally opposite to me, Introverted and a bit prickly. We'd clash often as I was all about the Customer and he was more about procedures and logistics.

I have one story that is my best experience in over 30 years in Sales. As I mentioned, the previous Manager was suppose to look after inner Slough. There was a big job happening in the main shopping centre in Slough. I kept seeing the cranes and often I asked Juan "what was happening about it"? His response was "don't worry about it, that's John's area"! After a few more months, I thought stuff this and drove up the ramp through the Boom Gates. I got out of my car and knocked on the site shed door and walked in and said "Gday, Nick from Edmundsons". Straight away I connected with both the guys who were the main two running the Electrical.

My timing was perfect as they literally had prepared the quotes for the other Suppliers. I took an "extra" envelope and jumped back in my car. I straight away realised I didn't have 20 pence to open the Boom Gates to get out. I jumped back out of my car and knocked on the door again. I walked in and they said, "what the fuck do you want now"? I explained my situation and they took the piss out of me and gave me the 20p and away I went.

After arriving back to the Branch, I spoke to Juan about the visit and luckily he knew one of the guys when he was working in London. The main bloke's name was Les Chadwick, a top bloke and a real Londoner. We spent a few days quoting the job and won it. The 20 pence got us £240,000 in Sales! I learnt so much with these two fellas and had many a good time taking them out on the drink. If only you had the chance to freeze those times and revisit them years later.

I was lucky to meet a group of guys who worked for the local electrical board. I still remember their names and sorry it may bore you, however they were a large part of my journey over there.

Dave Barwick, Mike Elcombe, Harry Sangha (H), Barry Harvey, Steve Lewin (Lew Lew) Ken Walker, Allan Pledger and Pete Sanders.

Every few weeks Juan and I took them to the local Club for lunch and beers. It was so much fun being with them and I never really felt like I was working!

Southern Electric or SEB as we called them were doing about £50,000 a year in Sales. When I left Edmundsons about 7 years later, we increased sales to over £400,000 annually.

Being so close to France, I convinced Juan to take our key Customers to Calais for the day. On one of our trips, a Customer Charlie, realised he forgot his Passport but somehow we managed to get him on the Ferry, how I am not sure? There were many moments like this when taking out such a large crew.

We caught a Ferry and it was beers straight away with a journey just over an hour from Dover. After our Ferry trip we went for Lunch and like always, such a laugh. Juan was always on guard as he was the Boss but I was just me and got stuck in with all the boys! After a "long" lunch we headed to the Bottle Shop/ Supermarket. The reason we were so keen to buy the booze in France was it's cheaper than the UK with Duty being taken off. When we eventually arrived back at Slough, all the boys were pissed as and had to unload their booze from the coach as their other halves picked them up. We did about 3 Trips to Calais with the Pinnacle coming up!

There were lots of stories with the SEB crew. The one that stood out the most was when I was on the Motorway, not far away from Heathrow Airport. I had a good view of Windsor Castle and noticed smoke as well as flames coming out of it. I was heading in to see the SEB boys and caught the small lift to their level. As soon as I got outside the lift, I looked out a large window and it was confirmed the Castle was on fire! I walked in quickly and said to the boys" Windsor Castle is on Fire!" They replied, "Yeh OZ (as they called me) we believe you". I said, "Fair Dinkum it is!" It was then, one or two came over to the window and called all the others over. The Office was about 3 to 4 miles away and it was the most incredible scene standing there seeing the flames!

MORE CRICKET:

That first Season at Boyne Hill was incredible. I batted number 3 and had my best results with the bat, scoring over 600 runs and averaged 45. We had a really good run of wins and all the bigger clubs thought we'd fall over at the last hurdle. Our 2nd last game was away to Tring Park and if we won, we'd be Thames Valley League Champions. We chased a lowish score and the two openers were going ok, although Nicky Watson was slouching along. When Shawy got out I walked out to the middle and said to Nicky, "get on with it or GET OUT, we need to win this today and not risk next weekend"! Nicky did get out trying to force the runs and we got home in a tight finish! We were TVL Champions and we celebrated in their Clubhouse and was presented the Winning Trophy and Flag!

Championship Team 1990. Sadly 3 are Deceased.

We partied all night back at the Club and unfortunately the next day we had to play a Friendly at Home. Jacko who was our opening bowler and the best Cricketer I played with or against in England. He got a Hat-trick with the first 3 balls of the game. To top it off, I wasn't Keeping but at 1st slip and took a one handed catch to my right for the third wicket and helped seal the Hat-trick. We went off and I am not sure to this day if the opposition knew how hard we partied the night before?

Not only did we do well in the main competition, we did really well in the Evening Competitions. The games started at 6 pm and went till 8.30/9.00 pm. I was lucky that as soon as I arrived at the ground, I was either Keeping or opening the batting. Our Club hosted one of the Finals and there were generally a min 150/200 people watching on. The Competition was called the Julian Cup and was recognised as one of the oldest competitions in the country. We won it 5 times!

My favourite pic. Running out a batsman after a difficult throw.

Like some sporting teams, they have Eras or "Purple Patches" and most of us were in our 20's. Our celebration drink was a mix of Port and Murphys, drunk from the Trophy. There was one night in our Celebrations and Amanda ended up in the shower (clothes on) with myself and Boycee!

Memories you can not get back, Amanda being drenched in her work Clothes with Boycee and me after another Evening Cup Win!

1993 Accepting the Julian Cup, great Memories.

A HISTORY OF
THE JULIAN CUP

1924 – 2004

80 YEARS OF LOCAL LIMITED
OVERS CRICKET

Julian Cup considered one of the Oldest Competitions in the World.

Champs retain their crown

The triumphant Boyne Hill side line-up for their victory team group picture after regaining the title they won last year. Pictured, back row (from left): Martin Porter, Steve Croxford, Chris Batt, Mark Watson, Mike Turner, Mark Smirnoff.

Front row (from left): Mark Turner, Richard Hobson, Nick Geale, Steve Palfrey (captain), Dave Shaw, Suhail Deen.

1994 Winners Again.

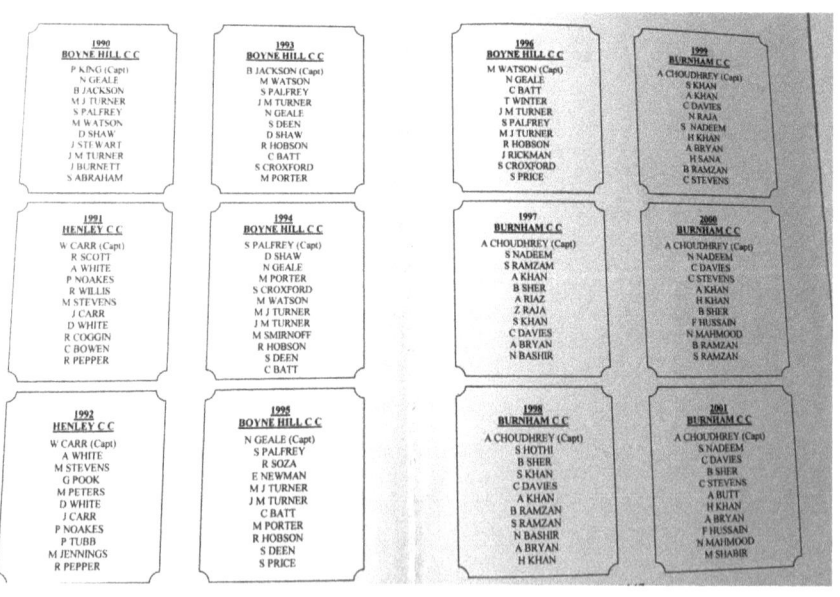

1990 BOYNE HILL C C	1993 BOYNE HILL C C	1996 BOYNE HILL C C	1999 BURNHAM C C
P KING (Capt)	B JACKSON (Capt)	M WATSON (Capt)	A CHOUDHREY (Capt)
N GEALE	M WATSON	N GEALE	S KHAN
B JACKSON	S PALFREY	C BATT	A KHAN
M J TURNER	J M TURNER	T WINTER	C DAVIES
S PALFREY	N GEALE	J M TURNER	N RAJA
M WATSON	S DEEN	S PALFREY	S NADEEM
D SHAW	D SHAW	M J TURNER	H KHAN
J STEWART	R HOBSON	R HOBSON	A BRYAN
J M TURNER	C BATT	J RICKMAN	H SANA
J BURNETT	S CROXFORD	S CROXFORD	B RAMZAN
S ABRAHAM	M PORTER	S PRICE	C STEVENS

1991 HENLEY C C	1994 BOYNE HILL C C	1997 BURNHAM C C	2000 BURNHAM C C
W CARR (Capt)	S PALFREY (Capt)	A CHOUDHREY (Capt)	A CHOUDHREY (Capt)
R SCOTT	D SHAW	S NADEEM	N NADEEM
A WHITE	N GEALE	S RAMZAM	C DAVIES
P NOAKES	M PORTER	A KHAN	C STEVENS
R WILLIS	S CROXFORD	B SHER	A KHAN
M STEVENS	M WATSON	A RIAZ	H KHAN
J CARR	M J TURNER	Z RAJA	B SHER
D WHITE	J M TURNER	S KHAN	F HUSSAIN
R COGGIN	M SMIRNOFF	C DAVIES	N MAHMOOD
C BOWEN	R HOBSON	A BRYAN	B RAMZAN
R PEPPER	S DEEN	N BASHIR	S RAMZAN
	C BATT		

1992 HENLEY C C	1995 BOYNE HILL C C	1998 BURNHAM C C	2001 BURNHAM C C
W CARR (Capt)	N GEALE (Capt)	A CHOUDHREY (Capt)	A CHOUDHREY (Capt)
A WHITE	S PALFREY	S HOTHI	S NADEEM
M STEVENS	R SOZA	B SHER	C DAVIES
G POOK	E NEWMAN	S KHAN	B SHER
M PETERS	M J TURNER	C DAVIES	C STEVENS
D WHITE	J M TURNER	A KHAN	A BUTT
J CARR	C BATT	B RAMZAN	H KHAN
P NOAKES	M PORTER	S RAMZAN	A BRYAN
P TUBB	R HOBSON	N BASHIR	F HUSSAIN
M JENNINGS	S DEEN	A BRYAN	N MAHMOOD
R PEPPER	S PRICE	H KHAN	M SHABIR

Julian Cup Winners in the 90's. We won it 5 Times, 4 in a Row 93-96.

Boycee was given his Nic name after an Actor in the series, Only Fools and Horses. Not only did he look like him with his "Tash", he was as "dodgy" as the fella playing Boycee in the TV Comedy. I became really close to Boycee and like a lot of my good mates, older than me. He came from a Village Cricket Club and he wanted to see how well he went with a better standard. There was a Sunday National Cup game and I was Skipper. He was late turning up and when he walked past me I said to him, "12.30 is fucking 12.30!" He still brings this up as a joke but appreciated I was trying to create a culture for consistency and success.

I got involved with the Club in a big way! I just loved seeing the Club develop both on and off the field. I was Captain of the 1st Team and was on the Committee. Like all Clubs there are generally only a few who get stuck in. The big plus about the Club was the numbers in the Juniors were very good. I put it to the Committee that we take a day off our own Cricket and give a day back to the Colts. The Committee was keen and I put the idea forward at a Player's Meeting and made it clear we all needed to help out.

We had our first Colts Day in May 1992. It turned out better than anyone ever imagined. My mate Rick played for us that Year and we set him up on the garage roof with a microphone and pumped beers into him all day. The Final was a nail biter and it became a yearly event. The fella who ran the Colts was a nice bloke. His name was Mike King (Kingy) once again older than me. We had so many laughs at the Bar, unfortunately he went through a messy divorce and he went downhill rapidly after that.

Boyne Hill CC before we planted the hedge.

Presentation Night with Boycee smiling with
his big tash and Mikey in the front.

Our main ground was fenced off in trying to keep the general public away. People casually walked on our square with their dogs and on some occasions never cleaned up their Mess. It however looked like a Prison Fence. I went to the Committee with the idea to plant a hedge in front of the fence. The Club was cash strapped and ran Financially on its own. Clubs here in Australia are generally owned and run by the Council.

I basically said we need to somehow find money to do this. I had vision of what it will look like in years to come and we managed to find some money. We purchased over 100 small Conifer trees and I had to get a few Members to help me with planting them. To this day there is now a beautiful hedge trimmed at fence height that looks fantastic. The older Members call it "Gealy's Hedge" which means so much to me!

*Rippa shot of Gealy's Hedge looking out from the Clubhouse.
The small picket fence is the corner of the Patio outside the
Club. It was built from the funds of Steve Palfrey (Palfs) after
he passed away and is dedicated to him, Great Bloke!*

*Me Keeping in my "Squat" position, know wonder my Knees
are Struggling! Notice the Fence in the Background!*

Man of Match in a Julian Cup Final. Taken approx 9pm.

As I mentioned previously, I was fortunate to score 10 Hundreds in my Career. Unfortunately, my highest score in the Saturday League was 90. I need to tell you about two of those Hundreds.

Not long after I arrived at Boyne Hill, we played a Sunday game in a town call Thame. We fielded first and was chasing a decent total. I went in just after 5pm and started to get into a rhythm and seeing the ball well. Amanda was with all the girls and giving some of the boys a haircut whilst they were waiting to bat. I got to my Hundred just before 7pm and continued to score 154 Not Out to Win the game. I was really lucky that our Scorer did a Wagon Wheel of my Innings.

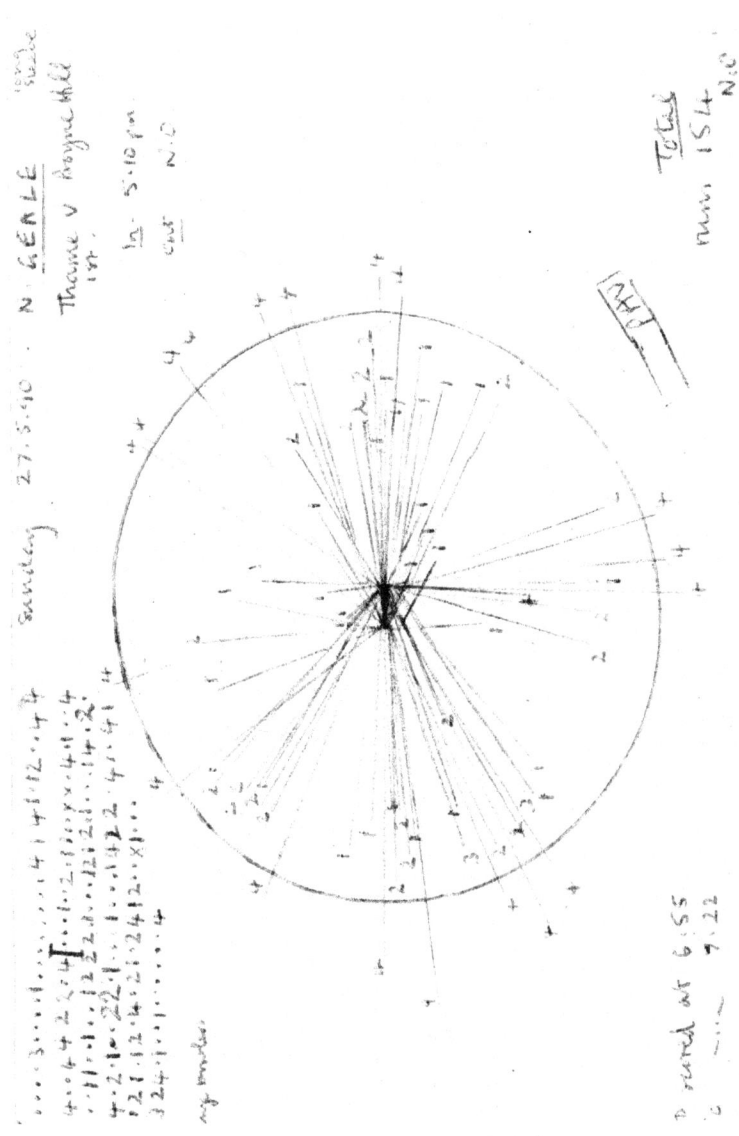

My highest score 154 Not Out, Priceless.

My other Hundred that needs mentioning was just before the start of our League Season in the early 1990's. I spoke to Tim through the week and he said he was playing Rugby close by on the Saturday. The last thing he said was "if you get a Hundred, I'll do a streak" and hung up the phone.

We were chasing over 200 and I came out at #5. I got to about 40 and Tim and Caroline arrived. Tim was walking around the boundary and kept giving me the "Thumbs up" ! I chipped away in 10's and in my 90's I lost sight of him. I was on 99 and knowing his personality I knew he'd do it! I punched the ball to Mid Wicket for a single to get my Century.! Straight away Tim bolted out of the Clubhouse stark bollocking naked! He jumped the closest set of stumps and hurdled the Bowler's ones and ran away up the hill. Like a true Professional he had his clothes tucked under his arms. Two years later when we played the same team at Home, they asked me if the "Nutter" was going to do the same again?!

This Painting means more to me than anything else, it simplifies our Great Game at the Club that gave me so many Memories.

SURPRISE:

So I think by now you have got it, Cricket was a big part of my life over there. Work was too and more importantly Amanda. On Valentine Day I receive a Fax attention to me. It read "Will you Marry Me"? Apparently every fourth year the Girls can "Pop" the Question. I casually sent the Fax back saying YES! I called back home to break the good news. Mum was really happy and I think deep down she thought, great another excuse to go back to the UK! The only thing I didn't do was to ask Amanda's Dad permission to marry his Daughter! Oh Well, he always took everything in his stride!

My Bucks Night, chained to the Bar! Year 1993.

It was September 1993 and Mum and Dad left for the Wedding. They went to Europe first and finally arrived mid September in Reading. I had already had two Bucks Days, one in Brighton and the other in Reading. The Brighton was a Rippa! We caught a "Dingy" mini bus organised by Willy and arrived in Brighton. The first Pub we went to was The Bulldog. I walked in and noticed the majority of them were blokes and the "Penny Dropped"! The boys cracked up and was a "stitch up" as they knew how'd I react! From there we walked into another and it was packed with Crowded House playing. It was Electric and finally arrived back to our Hotel in a real state!

We had another for those who didn't go to Brighton. I was in a dress and we jumped into a Mini Bus with Rednose, Tim and Lamby. Straight away a pair of Hundcuffs appeared and Tim asked, "who wants to go first?" Lamby agreed and one was cuffed on him and the other on me. Rednose straight away opened the window and Tim threw the key out! The look on Lamby's face was priceless and it was hilarious. Little did Lamby know, they had another key!

We went for the rehearsal midweek before the Saturday Wedding. Mum, Dad, Keith and Margaret was with Amanda and I. It was at the Church I heard we had just Won the Olympic Games bid in Sydney, Year 2000! The Church was in the heart of Reading, right next to the Prison which made me laugh!

It was drizzly on the Wedding morning and I still remember standing outside our little Maisonette asking above to dry up. My neighbour Mick was a good bloke and I asked him if he was happy to rent his place for the Weekend? Pes, Boh and Trudie stayed there with Mum and Dad in ours. We took a few photos outside before heading off to the Church.

Like all Grooms, I was nervous waiting for Amanda to walk down the Isle. Pes, Boh, Tim and Roy were my Groomsman and they kept me calm cracking jokes. Once Amanda arrived near me I was sweet. Tim and Caroline's boy Louis was dressed as a little Cricketer and Amanda's Neice's were with him as well as Hattie. Amanda looked amazing and I always will remember her looking at me with her vail on!

Outside the Church we arranged a Surprise for Dad. He spotted an old Morris Cowley similar to the one he bought and pulled to bits in his garage back home. Amanda and I got in and I don't know why I didn't ask Dad to jump in the passenger seat for the journey to the Reception, oh well.

Dad and the Morris Cowley, if only he had a ride!

Keith and Dad nailed their speeches and Pessy too did his best as Best Man. Our Wedding song was "I Had the Time of my Life", Patrick Swayze. After the earlier part of the Reception, all the boys arrived in the evening from Cricket and we all got on it! Margaret from #26 was there with her Sister Betty and they had a great time and still talk about our Wedding. Amanda and I stayed on the Premises and had a fantastic day!

Our Wedding day. Left to Right. Roy, Tim,
Dad, Pes, Me, Keith, Simon and Boh.

Left to Right. Aunty Ethel, Simon, Me, Amanda,
Karen, Margaret, Keith, Grandma. Below. Louis,
Hattie (Hidden), Bridie, Alice and Emily.

Married Sept 25th 1993.

Amanda went to see Madonna the next day and just after that we had another get together at Keith and Margaret's home. Amanda wore her Wedding Dress again and it was another top day.

HONEYMOON:

We arrived at the Airport and Amanda still didn't know where we were going. At the Airport I showed her the tickets and Tunisia here we come. Tunisia is located at the top of Africa, about a five hour flight from London. We arrived at our Hotel and were given a Surprise bottle of Champagne in our room.

Amanda and I chilling like normal at the Bar.

One of our highlights was going out in the Desert and visit the Nomads in their environment. They were so happy, showing off their small tents. It showed both of us that you don't need much and was an amazing day.

An eye opener, how simple Life can be.

It was such a relaxing holiday and we mainly chilled around our Hotel pool and I was drinking beers whilst Amanda was sun baking. We went into the town and bought a large vase that we still have to this day in our backyard.

Vase bought on our Honeymoon in Tunisia.

We were soon on our way home to England and were picked up by Amanda's Dad and her Uncle Pete.

It was back to reality with work for both of us, unfortunately the Cricket season was a good 6 months away.

ASHES 1994-95:

In the Season of 1993 Willy and I threw around the idea of a Club Tour to Australia with the Ashes just over 18 months away. The interest was really positive and we all got together for our first chat. We all thought spending Christmas in the UK was important and also cheaper for flights. This meant we'd miss the MCG Test but go to the last Test in Sydney. After the Test, head to Brisbane for a One Day game and off to Cairns and down to Melbourne for the Final.

So we had an Itinerary brief, so next Finances were discussed. It was decided that we set up a Bank Account for those "really" interested. The next issue was Fund Raising and lots of ideas were thrown about. At back of my mind I wanted something that was "Big" and out of the normal tried ways and kept thinking over the next 6 months.

In the following November, Amanda and I went to a Fire Works night with Tim and Caroline near where they lived. There were lots of people there and was good fun. In talking, Amanda said, "why don't you have one at the Cricket Club?" It was a Light Bulb moment and the next day I called Willy and he too thought a great idea as our Tour Fund Raiser!

After Christmas there was another get together with the potential Tourists. Willy and I put forward the idea of a Fire Works night at the Club for the coming November, just 6 weeks before the Tour starting. The enthusiasm was buoyant and we made it clear if we were to propose the idea to the Club it's one in all in, for helping on the night!

Willy and I went to a Committee Meeting and put forward the Fire Works Night. The Tourists were to run the Fire Works, therefore keeping costs down and it was agreed the Tourists to take 70% of the Profits and the Club 30%. The Fire Works Night was accepted by the Committee and the first Saturday in November was "Circled"!

Willy and I spoke on our home phones at least two/three times a week leading up to the Fire Works Night! We came up with a "Catch Phrase" with one word when either of us answered the phone,

"SPEAK"! A good 25 years later when we call each other from across the other side of the World, we still say "SPEAK", when answering!

Time was ticking and we made up a list of key areas that needed the most attention.

1. Fireworks/Bonfire and Safety.
2. Fun Fair, run by Outside Company.
3. Food/BBQ roster.
4. Beer Tent separate from Clubhouse.
5. Gate, Charging Entry Fee.
6. Donation Bucket on Hill, outside Fenced Area.
7. Club Bar Roster.
8. Tooheys Surf Board Tent.
9. Marketing

At least 3 weeks out from the night, the Bon Fire area started taking donated timber. It was located in the area called "The Folly" in between the two grounds. Come the Saturday morning, the Bon Fire was at least 6mts high and a good Soccer inner circle wide.

Ok, it was 5pm and everything was ready with our main concern being the Weather. Cars started to come in around 6 pm and parked on our 2nd Ground. It didn't take long before the allocated parking area was full and soon cars were banking up on the Bath Road outside the Club.

We were never really sure of how many people may turn up but being the Optimist, I had a real good gut feel numbers will be good! Families were arriving from the local area and the Hill started filling up!

The Bonfire was lit and a massive "Glow" was seen a good couple of hundred metres away down the Bath Road. The Bar and Beer Tent were filling up and the Fun Fair rides had lots of young children having fun. We had a few Tourists with buckets collecting Gold Coins with the visitors on the Hill.

Finally the time arrived to start the Fireworks with all the focus looking towards the Bonfire. Most of the Main Ground was Full and Yogi was on top of the garage roof located behind the main crowd. He was to set off the 1st Fire Work which I wasn't aware off. There was no count down and all of a sudden a "massive" explosion with everyone looking to the Sky at the 1st Fire Work "Launched" by Yogi!

Apparently "John Boy" went and did a one day "Pyrotechnics" induction course. Thank God he did! The years following the Club engaged a professional Company!

Fun Fair Rides, What a Night!

It was a very nerve racking for me leading up to the start but I sat back and enjoyed the next 10 to 15 minutes looking up in the Sky and thinking we have done it! There were a lot of estimates on the crowd and a conservative 2000 people was settled on.

We took £6490 and after Expenses the Tourist collected £1950 and the Club £835. Due to its success it has been a Yearly event and has turned around the Financial situation of Boyne Hill CC.

Boyne Hill CC Committee Meeting

2016 v 2015 Fireworks Display

GROSS REVENUE (exc VAT)	2016	2015
Main Bar (inc back bar)	2,060	1,746
Beer Tent	1,274	1,345
Hot Refreshments	595	250
Carters Food (mobile van) & Fair (ground rent)	1,200	12,00
Gate Receipts	12,234	6,280
Punt Hill Collection	2,022	1,912
	19,385	**12,733**

EXPENSES (exc VAT)	2016	2015
Fireworks	3,300	3,000
Barrier Tape	7	7
Security Personnel	90	135
Mobile Toilet	520	595
Maidenhead Advertiser	325	300
Hire of Beer & Refreshment Tents	0	150
Bar/Hot Refreshments Staff	50	80
Insurance (public liability and mobile toilets)	150	150
* Hot Drinks / Accessories	152	60
Veolia (hire of additional waste bins)	60	60
Cesspit (emptied before event)	175	171
Metal Stakes	30	60
Hire of PA Equipment	85	85
MET Medics – First Aid Cover	390	0
	5,334	**5,053**

PROFIT / LOSS ANALYSIS (exc VAT)	2016	2015
Main Bar (50% G/P)	1,030	873
Beer Tent (50% G/P)	637	672
Hot Refreshments	443	190
Carters Food & Fair (ground rent)	1,200	1,200
Gate Receipts	12,234	6,280
Punt Hill Collection	2,022	1,912
	17,566	**11,127**
Less Expenses (excluding *)	**5,182**	4,993

Best Year 2016, The Annual Fireworks Night secured the Club's Future!

There was one last get together at the Club just before Christmas and we had a nice photo out in the cold in front of the Clubhouse. We took off from Heathrow on Boxing Day and Australia here we come!

We had a hiccup on the way with our connecting flight to Sydney delayed at Bangkok. Finally we arrived in Sydney and my Family as well as Uncle Mick was there to greet us. He was our Mini Bus driver and we headed to Bondi stopping a few times for some Tourist Shots.

Taken just before Christmas 1993 with most of the "Tourist".
All Excited for the Ashes Tour in a week or so.

The next day we drove to #19 and I still remember jumping out of the Mini Bus and excitedly touched the new pavers that Justin had worked hard laying. The other Team that we were playing was also there, consisting of mostly mates of mine. We had a BBQ with Bacon and Eggs and some of the boys had a swim and soon after we took off to the Ground.

On our way to the Ground, we stopped to buy some ice for the Beers. We paid for about 6 Bags and we opened the door and I reckon about a dozen were thrown in. The Tourists loved it and we all cracked up!! It was hot and the Tourist bowled first. Pessy's brother "Corky" was opening the Batting with Yogi charging in. He nicked from memory his second delivery and Franky at 1st Slip dropped it! It was "electric" with everyone laughing and I'm sure still to this day everyone out there remembers that moment. The Tourist lost but Cricket was the Winner and we headed back to Uncle Mick's house for a BBQ.

We arranged to celebrate New Year at the top of our Hotel in Bondi. Unfortunately after about an hour, Security came up and said it was

unsafe and we had to leave. Let's say our New Year was a disappointment as we spent it on the grass area above the Beach.

We all went to the SCG for the last Test and all the Tourist were
taken back with the Pavilion. We were all sitting near the Bradman
Stand at ground level with our red, white and blue tracksuit tops on. It
started to drizzle and we headed for some cover and an Aussie called
out, "throw them some soap"! Everyone cracked up and it was "Banter"
all day long between the Tourists and the Australian crowd.

We left Sydney and arrived at Brisbane to watch Australia vs
Australia A at the Gabba in a One Day Game. The Gabba in those days
is nothing like it is now days. You were able to walk around most of the
ground and it was good fun watching with Mac from Leeds as we both
got on the drink.

Our next stop was Cairns which was a good 2 Hours Flight from
Brisbane. Amanda and I decided to go on a Air Ballon ride and the rest
of the gang went White Water Rafting. Next Day we all went out on the
Barrier Reef on one of those massive catamarans. Everyone had such
a great time snorkelling, although Frankie not being a good swimmer,
got in a bit of trouble but was fortunate to have a few mates with him.

We had lots of laughs in Cairns but to me this was the funniest. As
a group we all agreed getting together once in Cairns for a nice dinner.
It was one of those fancy Nouvelle Cuisine Restaurants. On the menu
was Bullock Steak and quite a few of us blokes ordered it. Entrees
arrived and all the portions were small but we took it in our stride sali-
vating for the main course.

The beer and wine was flowing and the main courses started to
come out. Everyone who ordered Bullock Steak including myself were
shocked when our plates arrived. Try and imagine ham slices, that's
exactly how it came out. It wasn't the T-bone thick slab of meat that
most of us were expecting!

I sat back and thought to myself, this will be interesting how
everyone will react? Most took it well and had a laugh but John Boy,
Willy's Brother, true to form carried on like a "Pork Chop". To me it was
another experience and sometimes things never seem what you think!

On our last night in Cairns, England were playing Australia A and we were all going for England including me as we had tickets for the Final in Melbourne. It was a tense game and England lost! Everyone was a bit mellow as it meant they were out of the Tournament and the Final was between Australia vs Australia A!

We all had a massive night and our flight to Melbourne was quite early the next morning. We were running late for our flight and only that we were such a large group the plane waited for us to arrive. We took off for a 4 hour flight and we were all so quite as everyone was catching up on sleep.

There was another game vs Noble Park as one of their players Mark Smirnoff, played for Boyne Hill in our Season just gone. Once again the Tourists were on the other side of a Win and big Fletch lost a bet and had to "Streak" around the ground with the floodlights on. We were lucky that the Club had a Leagues Club on the same premises and we partied after the game.

A few days after, we all went to the MCG to watch the Day Night Final. There were a lot of young guys playing for Australia A who went on the represent Australia. Players included Ricky Ponting, Mathew Hayden, Greg Blewett and Gavin Robertson, who I played Reps with. Although England were not playing, we were lucky that the Australian Open was on next door. We were allowed to walk in and out of both Arenas without any hassles.

After nearly three weeks our Tour was over. Amanda and I went back to Sydney and the rest of them left Melbourne and headed back to London. It was so satisfying that a dream became reality and I am sure everyone on the Tour look back with fond memories.

NEW JOB:

I was the key Sales person for the business and I felt I wasn't really being appreciated and taken for granted. Anyone who has done Sales knows how hard it is to HUNT New Business, rather than just look after existing accounts. I had a meeting with Juan in his office and I finally cracked! I literally threw my car keys on his desk and they just missed him hitting the wall. I picked up my wallet and kept walking. He jumped in his car and found me walking down the A4 towards Maidenhead. He pleaded with me to get back in the car and I said NO. Time was up and after nearly 7 years my days at Edmundsons were over.

Boycee knew I was out of work and being a builder, he needed someone to give him a hand. He is a top bloke and a funny man and to work with him was great. We were having Smoko on his building site one morning and I opened my food. Wrapped with it was a tiny pair of boots, the ones you hang on your windscreen mirror. I said to Boycee, "these won't fit Edward" his son. He replied "mate I don't think there for me". The penny dropped and I called Amanda straight away. She confirmed we were having a baby!

I was lucky to get a job in the Sports industry working for a Rugby firm called Cotton Oxford. They sold into the Retail Shops but also via the Clubs who they Sponsored. I can still remember my first call in Hartford, north of London. It was a typical old fashion sports shop and I was upfront with the owner it was my first call. He was kind enough to give me an order for some rugby supporters tops and rugby shorts.

Their biggest team they Sponsored was Bath Rugby Club. I looked after their Team requirements as well as their Supporter's Shop. If anyone has been to Bath in the UK knows how great the place is. It has so much history and just a top place to visit. I also had the privilege to look after Harrods in London. Just visiting was fantastic but to sell into them was a great experience. Another iconic location I sold to in London was Carnaby Street and strangely the shop was called Soccer Scene.

Just outside London was Twickenham. Like Lords is to Cricket, it is the home of Rugby. The shop was huge as it needed to be large enough to cater for a Capacity of over 80,000 spectators. One of the most popular jerseys I sold there was The Barbarians. It's an old Team made up of International Players and generally played at Twickenham. All the players wore their own socks from either their Country of Origin or their Club Team. The jersey has the iconic black hoops on white.

NEW ARRIVAL:

It was April 1997 and Amanda went into a long labour. She was in Reading Berkshire Hospital and finally we were delighted in the arrival of a baby Daughter, Daisy. When I called Mum back home, she was really happy and asked me "do you know what day it is?" I said, "no". She said, "Anzac Day". I was confused with the time zone and my first thought was Daisy will have a day off every birthday, how good is that!

We brought our little bundle of joy home and like any new Parents, we went through some challenging but amazing times. We planned the Christening and Mum was quick to arrange another holiday with Dad. The Christening was such a great day. Having all the Grandparents in one place again since our Wedding was priceless. How lucky are we that across the other side of the world we all can get together and back in their day such opportunities were not possible.

Back to work, I noticed there was a position going at Canterbury. They are an International Sports Brand and I thought may have more opportunities than the smaller company. My area was effectively the South of England. I was lucky to go down to Kent and catch up with my Folkestone mates as well as selling into Shops down there. Coming from New Zealand, Canterbury also were big into Sailing. I'd sell a mixture of Sailing Apparel and Fashion into the Marine Chandlery shops.

They also were the Official Brand for the All Blacks. This meant I sold into the New Zealand Shop in Piccadilly London. There was also a big day out looking after some of the All Blacks who were on Tour. I picked them up just outside Heathrow where they were staying and took them into London to sign autographs at the New Zealand Shop. The Kiwis are very humble and hanging out with them was another great experience!

We also went to a Test Match at Twickenham vs England. After the game we went into the main area where all the players and their families gathered. There were Greats milling around, Andrew Mehrtens, Jonah Lomu, Zinzan Brooke, Tana Umaga, just to name a few. The main guy from Canterbury who looked after Europe was also there. He had an arrogance about him and I was to have that confirmed not long after.

Dad with Amanda and Daisy in London; flowers are for Lady Diana's Memorial at Kensington Palace, Sept 1997.

Daisy's Christening with Amanda and Me.

I often met up with my boss Phil Morgan who was a nice guy. Interestingly, things went a little quiet at his end and he asked me to come to New Zealand House in London. Like normal I got there early and laid out my stuff on the large table as I had lots to talk about. Before I got a chance to discuss things, Phil said, "Nick we have decided to let you go"! It was quick and he put his hand on my shoulder and said, "get Legal Advice!" That showed me he was only the messenger! No doubt his boss who I mentioned earlier played a part in the decision. There I was standing by myself in the middle of London in shock. The first person I called was Juan who worked close by. Although I left in tense terms, I always kept a friendship outside work.

I did take legal advice and after listening to me, the Solicitor explained the main issue was Canterbury never indicated they were unhappy with my performance at any stage. To sack me on the spot was not Legal. I was honest with myself and felt out of my comfort zone in a new industry but thought my Sales and efforts were ok. I agreed to take them on for Unfair Dismissal. I had a lot of Jersey and Clothing samples and had to take them back to Nottingham as part of the Settlement. Amanda's Father Keith came with me as support and oversaw the sample returns as well as drop off my car.

I was unemployed and thinking of my next step? I called back home and spoke to my Brother Anthony. In the conversation he said, "why don't you come back home"? It hit me like a tonne of bricks as I never considered it at all. That afternoon, I picked up Amanda from the Saloon and I had Daisy in the child seat. After a few minutes, I asked her if she'd come back to Australia? She didn't say no and I played it easy for a few days until revisiting it.

After a painful few days Amanda said, "Yes" in returning back to Australia! I can not remember exactly how we broached the announcement to her Parents but I can say that they supported the decision, albeit painfully so. The next nine to twelve months was all about organising the next chapter in our life.

AUSTRALIA VISIT:

Rather than arrive back to Australia without a plan we both thought that if I went back home for a quick trip, it may help things when the three of us eventually arrive. I spent a lot of time with Mum looking at existing houses. It was obvious most of them needed plenty of work and when we were sitting with the Real Estate guy, he asked "have you considered buying a block of land and build a new home"? I said, "no not really", however in the back of my mind I had my Cousins as Builders and Justin and I had our Trades. I called Amanda that night and asked if she rather'd an existing house with all the work needed doing or a brand new home? She liked the idea of a new home and it was decided to explore the situation further.

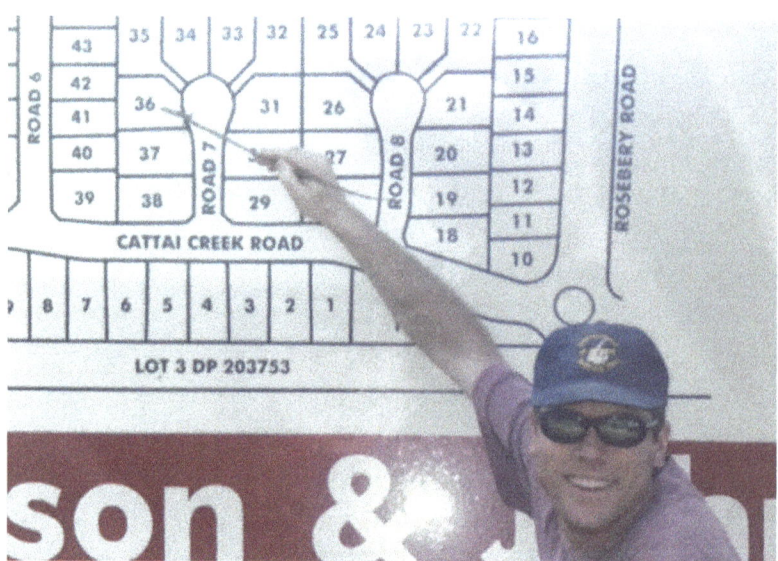

Proud Land Owners.

Mum and I met the Real Estate person in a suburb called Kellyville, not far away from Baulkham Hills. The land was still in its original state and we had to use our imagination and picture the future roads. I was keen to buy in a "coulda sac" as less traffic and safer for the children. We chose a block in a road called Sally Place. We paid $192,500 for a 652 sq/mt sized block and it basically took all our money up. So back on the plane to the UK to plan our return to Australia.

SAYING GOODBYE:

The next six months or so was a bit of a whirlwind. We decided to keep the small Maisonette and Rent it out, just in case things didn't work out. We sent most of our furniture back in a container and seeing the removal truck leave was emotional, especially for Amanda. I was working on a building site just around the corner so the money was still coming in. We had lots of emotional Goodbyes in the last month and both felt the clock ticking! We both wanted Daisy to have her 2nd Birthday with her Grandparents as well as Amanda's Brother and Sister.

Leaving Heathrow, Daisy, Grandad, Simon
and Jacob watching the Planes.

It was soon time to say goodbye. It was shocking and I have never felt so guilty! Taking away Amanda and Daisy from all of them was so Sad! We eventually went through the dreaded Departure section and left the tarmac heading for Sydney. The date was 1st of May 1999.

2nd Innings

When we arrived in Sydney my Brother Justin was there to pick us up. I still remember heading back to Baulkham Hills on Parramatta Rd and reflecting on what's to come. Mum and Dad were home when we arrived at #19. There was no big party, just a nice emotional hug to Amanda, Daisy and myself.

We were surprised with a purpose built door that separated Mum's kitchen to our living space in the Family Room, built by my Cousins. We had our own bathroom which I used growing up and our bedroom was at the end of the corridor. Daisy's room was opposite the bathroom which happened to be my old bedroom.

It was not long and we were asked to walk down to the garage. Being Jet Lagged, we just went with it and to our surprise there was a car sitting in the garage! Amanda's Dad Keith had sorted it with Jimmy Dobson at #26. We both cried with his generosity!

Within a few days we took a drive to see our new block of land in Kellyville. It did not have any curbing with only roads cut out. Trying to picture our Home in amongst all the works was a little surreal, especially for Amanda.

Amanda and Daisy out the front of our Block with the Car her Dad bought in May 1999.

As the weeks went by I started thinking about my employment. I got a job as a Sales Rep for a well known Electrical Wholesaler called JR Turks. I was looking after both the Castle Hill and Parramatta stores. I gave it a go but knew deep down I didn't really want to do it. Within about 2 months I was asked if I wanted to get into the Beverage Industry?

Boso had a contact at Spring Valley Juices and I met a guy named David Huxley at the Bull & Bush just up the road. We shook hands on a Reps role and I resigned from the Electrical Wholesale job. I went in to meet the HR dept of Spring Valley, thinking only a formality.

My first day I went out with a good young bloke, Dave Mullins. He took me on his run and I was taking in the products and the general role of what my job was to be. The very next day I was asked to come and have a chat with the fella who employed me, David Huxley. We sat down and he said, "there is a problem, HR don't think your suited for the job". I got emotional as I had gone through so much to get my Family back to Australia.

I said, "give me the Fucking Run and I'll go and Fucking do it straight away and I'll show that Fucking Bitch I can do it"! Most people are trained for a week and I had only a day! I only got half the run done that day but managed to catch up throughout the week. It's a classic example that these Bullshit HR people "Pigeon Hole" the "Norm" and have no idea really of the outside world!

I remember going home late on the second day and spoke to Amanda about what went on. I wanted her to know I'll do what ever it takes to get us settled into Life back in Australia. I was also very conscious of the Sacrifice Amanda made in leaving her family back in England!

Amanda enrolled Daisy in the Kindergarten just around the corner and the Mothers were allowed to come in and contribute. It was a nice way for her to slowly settle in and meet a few other Mums. Remember the motor bike story, the Kindergarten was built on top of the track. Daisy was such a gregarious toddler, always smiling or singing and was such a beautiful little girl. She was lucky to have Hannah, the youngest of Justin and Kathy's girls to play with. Dad loved taking them both to feed the ducks and give Amanda some time for herself.

We soon started to talk about the house to build on our block. My Cousins had started their own Building Company and they generously offered a very good deal on a "cost plus" situation. I was really conscious of their generosity and asked them to show us a home that they had built for a similar budget.

It was December 1999 when our concrete slab went down. The frame was next to go up in February and when I was working one day I had a nice visit from a fella who climbed up the ladder. He said, "hi I'm Peter and we are building opposite". I knew straight away he'd be a good neighbour.

Amanda was quite excited choosing all the colours etc and I was keen to let her take ownership. The biggest decision was the kitchen and around May it was installed. When Amanda walked in to see it she cried. Ken from across the road at #26 had a Kitchen Company and there was no one else who was to build it.

I did all the electrics and Justin was generous to do the plumbing and any time you build there are always some interesting moments. One day Justin was on a small ladder and it collapsed. He cut his hand trying to break the fall and had to go to hospital to get it stitched up. Another time, I noticed an electric lead plugged into my electric box. I followed it for a good 40/50 metres and came to a home where a young Carpenter was working. He was embarrassed getting caught out and I said, "mate, no worries using my power but please ask me next time".

Another funny moment was when I hooked up the electricity and started checking on things. Yes Murphy's Law, some of the kitchen and dining room lights did not work! I said out loud, "why me! in my own house" and a few people laughed who were there. It was an easy fix but I still laugh to myself years later.

Amanda's Father Keith, generously offered to help do the painting. He flew over by himself from England and stayed with us at #19 for about two weeks until it was painted inside.

Standing in the back corner near the Alfresco area,
great Memories!

NEW HOME:

We moved into 6 Sally Place on July1st 2000. We never had a fence and
it was one of the first things to be done for Amanda to fill safe. Quite
often she'd be looking outside and a random Tradie was walking past.
Once all the fences were up, our next job was to turf the lawns. Getting
the boys around and having some beers laying the grass was priceless.
Looking back, having the opportunity to see a home being built for
your Family is a great feeling.

I look at Mum and Dad's old photos of their Family home back in the 60's and it gives me a great feeling. They must have had the same excitement as Amanda and I had building years later. Dad was always coming up to help out and potter around as well as talk to our new neighbours.

The Rugby League Grand Final was earlier due to the Olympics. I was given a late ticket and went with all the boys. Seeing the New Olympic Stadium packed with 110,000 people was unreal. St George lost to the new team Melbourne in controversial circumstances.

In early September the Olympic Flame was run up Arthur Street, just around the corner of Mum and Dad's. We were so lucky with the route chosen and we cheered as it went past. There were people having picnics, toasting Champagne and having a great once in a life-time moment.

Amanda and I went to the "Rehearsal" of the Opening Ceremony. It was unreal seeing it as well as a privilege! We watched the Opening Ceremony at Justin and Kathy's house. Everyone was there, Mum and Dad, all the kids and some of their neighbours, what a great night.

Even though we went to the Rehearsal they kept the lighting of the Olympic Cauldron a big secret. We all know what happened that night, everybody was on tender hooks in suspense! Thank God it worked out.

December 2000 we had our 1st Street Party. Little did we know it was to be a Tradition to this Day! After a few drinks and playing in the Street when it was dark we went for a walk around the Streets to see the Christmas Lights.

Our 1st Christmas in Sally Place was soon upon us. Seeing Daisy running down the stairs and seeing what "Father Christmas" as Amanda calls him, was priceless. We showed her the Carrots and Water the Reindeer's had the night before and she was so happy open-ing her presents. It was also a happy and sad time for Amanda as she was so far away.

We headed over to Charles Street as Mum always had Christmas Day there. She spoilt the kids every Christmas with big bags full of presents. Uncle Mick, Melissa and David came over to join us for lunch until they were in their Teens. Mum's Christmas table was always great to see with lots of colour which rubber stamped her personality. Having beers under her huge umbrella out the back was always good fun. There were always lots of stories, some true and some not so true.

Around the time we moved in I gave up the Beverage job and went back into the Sports Industry. I was really lucky to get a job at Albion Hat & Cap Company. They made the "Baggy Green" for the Australian Cricket Team and also were the Pioneers into Helmet Protection

Originally they were heavily into Equestrian Helmets and when Rick Mckosker was hit and received a broken jaw in the famous 1977 Centenary Test, the Owner was listening on the radio. The Story goes that he turned the car around and went back to design a Cricket Helmet.

The shape was not too different to the Equestrian style, it was the face protection that caused the most difficulty. The original was a hardened Perspex face guard that sometimes made it difficult to see the ball. The next version was a steel grill and it was the version for over a decade or two.

Bat Signed by the West Indies Team. 3rd Signature
Brian Lara!

My keeping gloves signed by Jeff Dujon . No-one tried
my Gloves on, Sacred! Special as it is the same as the
original imprinted signature on the Gloves!

There were some good perks that went along with it. I was lucky enough
to be in the West Indies dressing rooms for a One Day International vs
Australia. I took a bat in hoping to be signed. When I asked the Manager
if it was ok, he said, "that's fine, it may take all day but all those others
laid on the table aren't going to be signed!" No doubt they get pissed
off with Companies assuming they will sign their bats! I was also lucky
to get my keeping gloves signed by Jeff Dujon who kept wicket for the
West Indies in the 80's and early 90's. He was in a training roll and as a
keeper too it was a special moment for me.

You'll notice a Jamaican Note attached to the top of the Bat. The
reason it is there is I asked the Boys what was the West Indies Currency
worth to the Australian Dollar? Jimmy Adams was there and asked one
of the Boys if they had any West Indies Notes. One of them pulled out

a Jamaican $100 Note. I can not remember the comparison but I can only think worth not a lot as Jimmy signed it and gave it to me.

They are a Fantastic Race, always smiling and happy to talk to you about Cricket. It's such a shame they are nothing like the Team in the 80/90's. Lets hope another Brian Lara, Viv Richards or Michael Holding can be found.

There was also an interesting moment when I took a phone call in the office from Steve Waugh. It was nice he remembered me from our playing days at Bankstown. He wanted to see if Albion was able to fix his "Baggy Green" cap? I arranged a time to meet him at his home to pick it up.

When I arrived his little girl was with him and he made a point of her saying hello to me which I thought was nice. We sometimes forget that these High Profile Sportsman are still Fathers or Mothers and are no different to us. He opened his garage door and dug into his Australian "kit bag" and bingo, out came the prized possession! All he said to me was "look after it" but unfortunately nothing was able to be done.

As you can see close up, his Baggy was wearing thin.

Steve Waugh's Famous Baggy Green.

Banktown District Cricket Club's 1st grade players and their numbers...

No.	Name	No.	Name	No.	Name	No.	Name	No.	Name	No.	Name
1	F. Johnston	41	N. Seach	81	M.C. Stephenson	121	F. Cicutto	161	N. Geale	201	J. Deitz
2	R. Amson	42	W. Pickles	82	P. Fitzpatrick	122	C. Heywood	162	G. Lovett	202	A. Smith
3	R. Briggs	43	A. Kelly	83	I. King	123	G. Irvine	163	D. Mitchell	203	S. Duff
4	G. Connelly	44	G. Sylvester	84	D. Madden	124	R. Bower	164	S. Sydes	204	D. Benson
5	W. Gibson	45	B. Webster	85	W. Palmer	125	L. Orlovich	165	W. Holdsworth	205	G. Roden
6	J. Giffen	46	R. Madden	86	K. Thorpe	126	I. Davis	166	S. Prestwidge	206	D. Sidie
7	H. Harris	47	J. Hickey	87	I. Gorman	127	K. Ferris	167	W. York	207	P. Clarke
8	E. Miller	48	C. Smithers	88	R. Lamaro	128	G. Spotswood	168	D.P. Waugh	208	M. Betsey
9	R. Nay	49	K. Gray	89	K. Jones	129	M. Vaughan	169	T. Cramer	209	P. Manistiotis
10	J. Theobald	50	N. Morrissey	90	L. Pascoe	130	P. Talbot	170	M. Freedman	210	V. Williams
11	B. Urry	51	A. McDonald	91	J. Thomson	131	A. Hamblen	171	B. Palman	211	H. Dannaoui
12	G. Allen	52	L. White	92	A. Radanovic	132	K. Everson	172	B. Hugo	212	D. Moy
13	R. DeFries	53	D. Bourne	93	I. Madden	133	P. Summers	173	S. Moss	213	T. Brown
14	W. Devine	54	D. Breeze	94	G. Heggie	134	G. Crowfoot	174	K. Hall	214	J. Allsopp
15	R. Duncan	55	R. Ingham	95	K. Scully	135	S. Smith	175	S. Thompson	215	C. Gane
16	M. Fox	56	D. Jones	96	J. Bull	136	B. McKirdy	176	M. Bartley	216	S. Jamieson
17	N. Holden	57	B. Bates	97	R. Grange	137	G. Tyndall	177	G. Cubitt	217	A. O'Brien
18	R. McHarg	58	D. Cathro	98	R. McDermott	138	L. Sterrey	178	S. Phillipson	218	B. Roworth
19	L. Thomas	59	R. Justice	99	R. Thebridge	139	G. Pride	179	S. Dignam	219	A. Bird
20	A. Asquith	60	G. McMillan	100	R. Holland	140	G. Hogan	180	S. Pope	220	M. Bright
21	W. Britton	61	P. Scahill	101	G. Robinson	141	T. Davies	181	R. Luc	221	C. Parkinson
22	N. Carroll	62	A. Taylor	102	K. Chevell	142	P. Kelly	182	S. Luc	222	C. Price
23	E. Condran	63	R. Pareezer	103	K. Robinson	143	G. Liddle	183	B. Elliott	223	P. Dugmore
24	K. Lang	64	D. Paull	104	K. Dixon	144	D. Thompson	184	C. Madden	224	G. Scuglia
25	G. Russell	65	K. Tyson	105	N. Girardin	145	I. McRae	185	D. Bull	225	D. Ettridge
26	N. Wright	66	J. Dunn	106	T. McDonald	146	P. Harmer	186	G. Trevena	226	J. Bourne
27	J. Clift	67	J. French	107	L. D'Costa	147	M. Willey	187	K. Roberts	227	B. Van Bier
28	A. Ellis	68	J. Corbett	108	A. Lamb	148	T. Sullivan	188	B. Smith	228	P. Darwen
29	P. Power	69	G. Doyle	109	R. Wyatt	149	M. Waugh	189	S. Vidler	229	G. Atkin
30	W. Silas	70	K. Ferguson	110	L. Andrews	150	S. Waugh	190	D.J. Waugh	230	S. Keen
31	L. Smith	71	H. Bunton	111	C. Jones	151	G. Briggs	191	S. Grant	231	D. Burns
32	J. Fitzpatrick	72	W. Boardman	112	M. Fisher	152	S. Green	192	N. Bracken	232	C. Small
33	J. Urry	73	R. Byrne	113	S. Small	153	G. Swanson	193	S. Deitz	233	C. Ridley
34	D. Rixon	74	R. Erickson	114	J. Brand	154	A. Divall	194	T. Woodhill	234	B. Van D
35	D. Stanley	75	G. Hinks	115	G. Pitty	155	C. Sinclair	195	C. Richards	235	S. Truesh
36	G. Thomas	76	B. Lewis	116	G. Thorpe	156	P. Vidler	196	S. McKiernan	236	M. Polso
						157	S. Cyriak	197	D. Mapee	237	A. Sams

Cap Numbers for Bankstown CC. Note, No's 90 & 91, No's 149 & 150 and Lastly No 161.

My Bankstown Cap #161.

When I was there, Albion was creating a Plastic style helmet that was different to the traditional cloth covered fibre glass version. Mark Waugh was invited to come in and offer his opinion. He was very positive with the new style and was to wear it later in his career.

Albion was struggling with profitability and they appointed a female to turn things around. She was an interesting piece of work, nice to your face but always had a hidden agenda. A lot of people were moved on and I never trusted her. I made up my mind to search for something else.

I always had a hidden ambition to have my own business and I met a guy who had his own Electrical Contracting business at Castle Hill. We both clicked and I decided to leave Albion with the opportunity to maybe Invest in the Electrical business. I made it very clear that I had been out of the Trade for over ten years and it may take some time settling back in. Things started out ok and I was on the tools as it was thought the best way of getting the respect from the other workers.

As time went on it was becoming clear the Owner expected more from me and one morning he brought it up. The scene was extremely tense and I decided that the best way was to leave immediately. I had to be honest with myself and back on the tools after such a long time, was a stretch too far!

I walked to the local News Agent and bought a paper and when I finally got home after a long walk I told Amanda what happened. After settling down, I went through the job section and there was a position going for a Manager of an Electrical Wholesaler at JR Turks Brookvale, yes the same company I left a few years back.

I went for the interview and before I knew it, I was the Manager. Normally anyone who becomes Manager has worked their way up and knows the computer system backwards. In all my previous jobs I've never had to work a computer, so the step was massive. I was seen as a bit of an outsider and it was difficult getting the team coming with me. The three main guys were post 40 and set in their ways which triggered a few ding dongs on the way.

Within the first few months of arriving we had a stocktake. There was a large discrepancy with a loss of approximately $40,000. Although

I liked my Boss, I felt I was going to take the blame for it. There was a roving guy who also had plenty to say and there was a meeting arranged in my office. I sat behind my desk and as I thought it was skewed to be my fault. I exploded and said, "there is no Fucking way I'm taking any responsibility for this!" I knew deep down someone was covering up and I just stood my ground!

The biggest customer was treated like a God. As I looked into his account it was clear he was using us as a Bank and paying in min 90 days. This had been going on for years and to add to the situation my Boss had a good relationship with him. I questioned, "why are we running around for this company who pay late and others who pay on time are treated less?"

I tried to get new business and was introduced to the owner of a well known company who had a good name. His name was Steve and we clicked straight away and he bought more and more on a monthly basis.

NEW ARRIVAL:

Amanda and I went to a Wedding in the Church at Oakhill College. She was heavily Pregnant and as we were walking up the stairs, a bloke asked, "how long to go?" Amanda replied, "4 weeks" and he said, "are you sure" and we all had a laugh. After the Service we headed back to Sally Place to kill some time before the Reception.

I was outside on our driveway and a neighbour down the road came up for a chat. We were both talking and Amanda said, "Hi" from our upstairs bedroom window. Literally just after she said, "Fuck, my water just broke"! Don't forget, this was 4 weeks early and we didn't have anything organised, not even a baby bag. I took Amanda to the Hospital which was luckily only a 10 min drive. She was very uncomfortable and here "dignity" was tarnished as she walked from the car park to Reception.

She was soon in a bed and a lot more comfortable wearing a dry hospital gown. It was then we started talking about a name for our soon 2nd baby. We somehow had a small book with names, I can only think Amanda must have had it in her handbag. We were going through the Boy names and got to the Letter H. First one that came up was Harry and we both said, "Nah" as my Dad's name is Harold. Next was Henry and we both liked it and agreed on it if a Boy. To be honest, I cannot remember a Girl's name and as it turned out it wasn't required.

It was 15th Sept 2002 and we were gifted with a baby Boy! Henry was born and after our cuddles he went straight away into an "Incubator." The rest of it is a "blur" but Daisy had a little mate to play with.

Henry on his Christening Day.

We had a Christening at the Church which happened to be the one I worked on as an Apprentice all those years ago. Justin was standing with the other Godparents near the Alter and he noticed they were all holding a Candle. He stepped forward and "Whispered" to the Priest, "I haven't got a Candle". The Priest was holding a Massive one and said to Justin, "you can use this one". So there was Henry's Godfather Justin, holding this massive candle looking a little embarrassed, everyone had a laugh!

Uncle Justin holding a Borrowed Candle!

After the Service we all went back to Sally Place for a Party to Celebrate Henry David Geale's big day. We had a small marquee and also got a jumping castle for the kids and as the beers flowed the Adults had a go.

LIGHT BULB MOMENT:

After about 20 months working at Brookvale the Assistant Manager's job became available. There was a fella I interviewed who left a Multi National Competitor under questionable circumstances. In the meeting I asked him about the town of Windsor as I knew he'd have some knowledge on. In the back of my mind I thought of getting closer to home and open another branch for JR Turk. He said, "it's the most profitable Branch in the Group!" After the meeting my Boss swung past on his way home for a beer and asked how the meeting went? Within the chat I brought up the Windsor discussion and mentioned what I was told. My Boss's reply was the "Catalyst" of me Opening my own Electrical Wholesaler! "Oh don't worry, there are only two main customers out there!"

It was "that comment" a "Light Bulb Moment" occurred and I thought, why can't I open one myself? I drove home that night and as it was a good hour plus drive the idea became bigger and bigger! I arrived home and spoke to Amanda about the meeting and my Boss's comment. I came out with it and said, "I want to open my own Shop!" She said, "yeh why don't you look into it"?

The following weekend was the June long weekend and we went for a drive with Daisy around the Hawkesbury area. I borrowed a Yellow Pages book from Jim Dobson who owned a car yard in Richmond, the next Town on. My main concern was to see if there were any other Independent Electrical Wholesalers in the Hawkesbury.

On our way back from Richmond, I was heading through McGraths Hill and I knew it as Ken Dobson from Charles St owned a Kitchen Company there. We were on Windsor Rd heading away from Windsor and I was thinking about easy access for the Electricians. I turn't right at a major intersection with traffic lights called Groves Ave. As we drove along it I noticed some Industrial Units being constructed. We turned into the Complex and cruised slowly towards the end unit. Luckily the roller door was half way up and we drove straight into it. I stopped the car in the Warehouse and turned to Amanda and said, "why can't I do this"? Once again she had a positive response and said, "yes why not"?

I called the Landlord and arranged a meeting early on the Tuesday morning. Within a few minutes I said to him, "I'll take that one"! He was a little taken back with the hastiness and agreed to hold it for a few weeks. It was June 2003 and I was on my way to fulfil my inner ambition of having my own Business.

The next few months sorting everything I "thought" was the most stressful time of my life. Unfortunately it was not, more on this later. I was very aware not to talk to too many people as I was working for a Competitor and also I did not want the Industry to know until I was ready to announce it.

I called Juan in England one night letting him know the exiting news. He was obviously wrapped with it and after a long chat I put the phone down. I reckon it was less then two hours later and the home phone rang. It was Juan and for some reason I knew what he was going to say. He said, "what if I help you?"

I was so taken back and the answer from me was "Yes, thank you!" At that moment it became more then just maybe it might happen, to more like, it's going to happen!

MELBOURNE:

In the July of 2003 we got some bad news that Rick's Brother Darren had Melanoma Skin Cancer. Boso, Robbo, Mads and myself, whom all played cricket with Darren, went down to see him. We all went to the AFL on the Saturday night and later off to the Casino. It was great seeing Darren smiling and appreciated his old mates all together. There was a classic moment after we were leaving the Casino. I needed a "slash" and spotted a dust bin with a small opening. I started "relieving" myself and the boys asked "where's Gealy?" They spotted me and rushed over and got me in a taxi before Security got me!

On the Sunday we went to Mike and Joan's house and spent the whole afternoon drinking beers and telling old stories. Rick and Janine were there with their three children. Sadly the two eldest, Caydn and Keelin suffer from a Muscular Disorder which means they are wheel chair ridden for their entire lives. The youngest Emmerson was lucky not to have the same Gene deficiencies and has a normal life ahead of herself.

Nursing Keelin, Caydn is holding the Phone!

Rick and Darren's sister Meagan was also there with her Husband and young kids. He played Test Cricket for Australia, Mathew Elliot. Darren was also a really good cricketer, playing 1st Grade in Melbourne and Perth.

Classic Pic in the Foley's Bar. I spent many a time there when Visiting Foles. Billy, Mike, Dazza, Robbo, Brian, Foles, Me, Mads, Boso.

Darren, Danni and their Daughter Mia came over and hanging out with the Foley Family was an unforgettable experience! We had a great "priceless" photo taken upstairs in the bar and it was soon time to leave. We were all out the front gathering around to say goodbye. Seeing Rick's kids in their wheelchairs and heading up the ramp into his van was shattering. It was an extremely sad time and my thoughts were not just for Darren and Rick's situation but also for Mike and Joan, their Parents. They are the most beautiful and so down to earth people who had a lot to do with me growing up!

I got a lift to the Airport with Mike and Darren. I kept my emotions in check as best as possible. I said goodbye and the "last words" Darren said to me from about 20 metres away was," Good Luck with your New Business Gealy!" I have never forgotten those words and whenever I was down, I'd go back and remember his Words! Unfortunately Darren passed away over a Year later, it was another Sad visit to Melbourne!

NEW BUSINESS:

The next person I told was Pommy. He had his "Business Head" on as normal and started asking me lots of questions. It was very clear that I needed to do a proper Business Plan and Pommy said he will help. We spent about two to three weeks on it outside business hours and there was so much to go through and take in.

We did the normal SWOT analysis, Strengths, Weaknesses, Opportunities & Threats. He worked for Lend Lease and previous to that, Ernst and Young. His detail with putting the Business Plan together was a real experience! After going through the process, Pommy said he will invest. So that made three including myself but I was keen to get someone to actually work in the Business and also have "skin" in the game.

There was a guy Managing another branch of John R Turks in Sydney who I clicked with straight away. Chappo and I caught up for a coffee and as I trusted him, I just came out with"I'm going out on my own"! I said, "I want you to come in" and he was totally taken back by what he just heard!

Unfortunately after going backwards and forwards over the next few weeks, Chappo pulled out. I was still keen to get extra investment and I approached my Cousins as they were Builders and I thought may be an asset and not forgetting good blokes.

We still didn't have a Name and it was one evening I was talking to Pommy on the phone and I said, "I want the Business to be recognised in the same way John Symonds is with Aussie Home Loans". Pommy said, "why don't you call it Aussie Electrical?" Straight away I knew it was the one and locked it in.

We had a few meetings with my Cousins and they decided to come on board with a few provisos. Andrew said, "we don't want you to think of our Investment as a gift" and I understood exactly what that meant. They also did not want any undue pressure put on their current Electrician doing their homes. I didn't think it was a big thing and thought he'd understand the Company that gives him all their work, he'd reciprocate. As it turned out it was a huge mistake and being inexperienced and so close to them, I didn't want to rock the boat so early!

It was about June/July when I put my notice in with my current

Employer and I said I was going to a Competitor. I was asked to leave immediately and caught a bus from Brookvale to Sydney CBD. That journey was so weird as I knew I was entering a new stage in my life. I also understood that I was the one who had to perform for the Investors! I arrived at Australia Square and caught the lift to the floor of Lend Lease. Pommy came over and twigged why I was there and I said, "let's go!"

The next month was full on with organising what needed to be done. Here are the main things to set up our Business in no particular order.

1. Staff
2. Stock/Suppliers
3. Racking
4. Bank
5. Vehicles
6. Fitout
7. Insurance
8. Marketing
9. Computers
10. Phones

I also read a great book from Richard Branson and his success with Virgin. He has 4 key ingredients to a successful Business. As you read my story, numbers 3 & 4 were my most Vulnerable.

1. Good Business Plan
2. Believe in your product/brand
3. Have good people around you
4. Limit your downside

Unfortunately Pommy was enticed to go and join a New Start up himself in the UK in the September of 2003. So it meant two Directors were in the UK with my Cousins and myself in Australia. Regardless, it was myself only working in the Business and the other 3 Parties sitting on the Sideline. I didn't really understand the enormity of what I was taking on and keeping it a secret to the Industry was extremely stressful.

Not knowing if there was also to be a new Competitor Opening close by, was an underling horrible feeling.

About half way between Kellyville and McGraths Hill, I kept driving past a long wire fence on a large property. I envisaged a massive sign and eventually stopped just inside the gate. I walked up the driveway and I knocked on the door and I met a lovely elderly couple. I explained my situation and if they were ok for the sign and offered them a monthly cash figure. They immediately said Yes and I asked them their names, Lowla and Mervin.

Sign on Windsor Rd, Sept 2003.

Dad with Suzanne and Scott, just before Open Day.

Ready for Trade, Dad helped with our Cleaning for a good few years!

OPEN DAY:

Finally after all the hard Prep Work, on the 1st of October 2003 Aussie Electrical & Data Supplies opened it's doors. I still remember looking down the driveway to the gated entrance of our Units on Groves Ave. It felt really surreal and it was still sinking in. We employed a young fella who had an Electrical Trade, Scott. I also employed a friend of the family to help with Accounts part time, Leisa.

We were given a contact from our Accountant, Kim. She was to do our Bookkeeping and she had a friend who was looking for work. Her name was Suzanne and came from James Hardy and I said to her "you will get bored!" Her personal situation had changed and was keen to start. Both Leisa and Suzanne were part time and Scott was full-time. As I needed to go out and hunt New Business I employed another guy named Dave.

I still remember our very first Sale. A plug and socket to put onto an extension lead. He wasn't an Electrician, his name was Guy. Roll on 15 years and we still talked about "that Sale"! I called my Cousin's Sparky if he liked the idea of being Customer #1? He quite liked the attention.

In our 1st month, Aussie Electrical Sales were only $9000. I knew for a fact that Sales in two other "Start Ups" were 150k and 180k in their 1st Month. The reason they were so high was they had worked for Multi National Competitors for 10/15 years and brought across Business.

The other side to this is probably the most important; the Business they brought with them was "Good" Business. There was no way they'd risk bringing "Bad" or "Slow" Payers to "their own" Businesses. Stress Levels were so much different than mine! They were busy getting deliveries out, where I was busy trying to get Business in.

Doing my time in the UK and only a short while at the Beaches, meant I didn't have the luxury bringing "any" Business with me. I had an extremely tough road ahead and I was hoping that Customer #1 was going to give us the kick start we needed!

The next few months I spent introducing myself to the Electricians in the Hawkesbury area. Being a new player took time and I knew what "Hunting" takes, Time! Most of the Electricians were using the two Major Companies across the way. I was hoping they might use Aussie on Route on the other side of Town. I did hear of a few Sparkies using another Independent but didn't think they were as big a threat as the Majors. Little did I know the Independent was to become a huge problem in years to come!

We had a belated Open Day in early December and only a few Sparkies turned up. It was mainly family and friends that came along to support. We had the local radio there and Michael Dobson from #26 got dressed up as Santa Claus for the kids. One of the Sparkies was Scottish and came along dressed in his kilt and played the Bag Pipes. It was good to announce ourselves, albeit in a small way.

A Bunnings store was being built around the corner and we were lucky that the Electrical Company who won the work was willing to give us a go. It definitely helped in those early months but years later it became obvious that being so close to Bunnings was hurting us in a big way. Even Electricians were going into Bunnings and buying Cable, Conduit, Power Points, etc.

*Santa has Arrived, my Dad is holding the Box, as you
can see we were a long way off the Road.*

*Open Day Dec 2003, my Mum always said
how "proud" she was that I had a Go!*

The hardest Supplier to secure was Clipsal and although I had a good
relationship with the Regional Manager Skewsy, we had to bide our
time. It was then I started learning about the Politics that existed in the
Electrical Industry. I know the Majors were not happy with more and
more Independents opening up.

Skewsy was helpful in introducing me to a local Electrical
Contractor. Without naming the Company for Legal reasons, I started
to form a reasonable relationship with the Owner. Although I had a

good 10 years behind me in Experience, working the Egos of some of these Owners was becoming a real challenge!

It's funny how there seemed to be an underlying "Pecking Order" ie

Builder,

Electrician,

Wholesaler,

Manufacture.

I never ever thought I was any better than the Manufacturers I purchased from. I treated them as important as my Customers and always welcomed any Sales Reps who popped in to see Aussie Electrical.

I remember asking a "walk in" Customer one day what he did for a living? He said, "I'm just a Driver", I replied "no, your not just a Driver, without you I can not sell any of these products on the shelf"! He smiled and walked away feeling better than when he walked in.

There was one young Electrician who's Account Number was in the 30's which indicates he signed up in the earlier days. I started to get to know him quite well and he too felt good about doing Business with us. I will revisit this Electrician throughout this book and will only refer to him as #30's. So already you have been informed about 3 Companies without being named, which in itself indicates trouble ahead!

We had our 1st Birthday at the Branch and a Sydney Radio Sports Show did a Live Broadcast. Robbo, who I played Cricket with and went on to play Play Test Cricket was on the Show, so too was Graeme Hughes who played 1st Grade Rugby League and Shield Cricket. The third Sportsman was Brett Papworth who played Rugby for the Wallabies and 1st Grade Rugby League! It was a top afternoon and lots of Electricians and Tradies came along.

There was an hilarious moment when we "set up" the boys whilst "On Air"! I had arranged for some ladies to come along and mingle with the Tradies. Yes, ok they had their tops off but it's a Male dominated industry and there were no other Females around. I asked the girls to go over to the table where the show was being broadcasted. They were talking to callers and concentrating on them. It was then one of them looked up and started laughing at what he was seeing. The other panel members too looked up and all were stunned and found it really funny. It was "harmless" and the girls took it in good spirit and in their stride!

Although Sales may have been better, I really thought we had made good progress in our first 12 Months and the foundations, albeit small we're starting to be laid. We had really good structure and link up phone calls to the UK with all Directors was a bimonthly event. We went over the Sales generally first up and then onto Profit & Loss reports. My Cousins were foreign to P&Ls and they really started to appreciate how important it was to see how we were tracking!

Pommy was all over the Reporting as he did it for a Living and Juan had a good 10/15 years behind him working for the big boys in the UK. For the first 12/18 months those meetings were straight forward as everyone knew we were a "Start Up" and will take time. Things started to "Heat Up" when our Cash started to dwindle and the Business was not where we all wanted it to be.

Our Expenses were quite high as we Invested in a Industry Leading Computer Software as well as the normal fixed Costs, Wages, Rent etc. We tried to maintain a GP% of 25% as we knew was an Industry Standard. This also meant we didn't go down the Route in Selling inferior Imported Products as we wanted to be seen as a Reputable Player!

It took about 2 years and finally we had a direct account with Clipsal. I shook Skewsy's hand and said, "we will not be going down the line of Cheaper Power Points and Light Switches". Little did I know that a lot of our Competitors were and started to win over the smaller Electricians with Cheaper Imported Products!

The Residential Customers were not aware they were getting Cheaper Brands installed and still being charged Premium Prices. I actually caught out an Electrical Contractor doing just that. We were in my Showroom face to face and yes I Apologised that it was Unprofessional of me exposing him. I stood my ground as I knew he was in the wrong! Roll on about 10 Years, I bumped into one of the Electrician's Builders and he noticed what was going on and questioned him. The Sparkie replied with, "I thought you only meant the Power Points" and the Builder replied with, "no everything"! The Builder stopped dealing with the Contractor!

The same Electrical Contractor was on the front page of the Local Paper "winging" that a Local Builder went broke on him for approximately $200,000. He was able to keep "Trading" by "Milking" the Imported Products, and therefore was "banking" the Residential Customer's higher profits, Grub!

I tried to win over the Electricians with better Service and also Referring work to them.I remember one Electrician came in only to buy a Book for Electrical Standards. I was the only one in the area that had them and at the Counter I quietly asked why he didn't consider Aussie. He came out with, "You've already tried to give me work" in an Arrogant voice. I felt so "Flat" as he walked out thinking, why do these Sparkies think they don't need Referrals? There were a few Loyal ones that understood my Strategy but there were lots out there that didn't care about Referrals and Quality.

Everybody invested $100,000 at the start and as I mentioned cash was decreasing. We all invested another $50,000 around year 3 and I was hoping that was enough. It was around that time when I made a visit to a local Water Treatment Plant. There was a Sparky doing some work and like normal I walked over for a chat. I introduced myself and the talk was easy, his name was Jim. He was employed by Sydney Water and I thought just another visit that may not go anywhere.

Roll on about six months and a Ute parked outside the Branch with the name, Jim Douglas Electrical written on it. He had left Sydney Water and went out on his own and came to enquire about opening an Account. My answer was a definite "Yes" and it was the start of a Business relationship and developed into a true friendship! When I really got to know him it was obvious he was not a typical "House Basher" type Electrician who only did Residential work. He was an allrounder who took on anything that came his way. The other thing that I discovered early, he had a fantastic sense of humour and was always fun when he visited Aussie!

Jimmy was a Classic, he just has the "Knack" of making you Laugh!

NEW IDEA: # 1 - ONLINE SHOPPING.

Within the first twelve months I was approached by a new Online Company who specialised in Electronic Shopping Carts. It was early days in Online Selling and after a few meetings we decided to invest approx $5000 into it.

We decided to target the Retail Customer as we didn't want to "upset" our Electricians who were already dealing with us. In simple terms, we were selling a Power Point on our Shopping Cart Site for $12.50/15.00, rather then $7.50/10.00 which was approximately what the Sparkies were paying.

We were getting some Sales but it wasn't getting the momentum that we all wanted. We persevered, letting it "jockey" along. Leisa was in charge of loading all the products with myself indicating price points.

Our 1st Online Shopping Site.

As it turned out the three main guys who owned the Technology pulled out of the Business and only one person was left to run it. Being so early in the Online Market meant we may have chosen a Company that too were learning on the go and this had impact on Sales and Investment.

It was about 4/5 years later and I took the Family to the Snow for a small break. I was on a chair lift and met a bloke who had a friend who owned a Shopping Cart Business. I gave him my number and a few weeks later I met up with him. His name was Peter and after looking into our current Online Cart, he explained why it wasn't getting the traction we were expecting. He put forward a quote and we all decided to give it a 2nd go. We were attracting about 5% of our Revenue with the Online Shop but even with our 2nd attempt I again felt disappointed with the take up. There was a 3rd attempt that I will revisit later.

NEW IDEA: #2- MOBILE ELECTRICAL SUPPLIES.

With Pommy's Lend Lease days we were privy to be tipped off about a massive new Town Centre to be constructed at Rouse Hill. It was one of our "Key" reasons for Opening in the North West of Sydney. I was given the name of the person who looked after Asia Pacific for Lend Lease, Eng Oh. I sent him an email expressing our interest on the new Town Centre and my relationship with Neil Jones (Pom). He came back to me and pointed me in the right direction to the fella who was Head of Contracts and was overseeing the Rouse Hill Project.

There was a "Light Bulb" moment around 2005 when I was on the phone to Chappo. I was trying to find a specific part and with JR Turks Branch Network it was easy to find items. Chappo who was Managing Castle Hill said,"my Computer System was down and call back later." I put the phone down and said to Scott, "their Computers are down." Scott's reply was, "why don't we fill up our van with stock and park it outside Turks?" He did not realise the impact his words made on me and I wrestled with the idea to start a Mobile Electrical Wholesaler.

The Hawkesbury was like most Rural Towns and the Locals generally preferred to support their own. It took me a while to work out that I was an Outsider and although no one really said it, I understood their parochialism.

I called Juan about the idea of going to the Sparkies with a Mobile concept. He was like always, conservative on his thoughts but understood my concerns attracting New Business.I brought up the idea at our next phone link up with all parties and it was decided to give it a go.

We had bought a Renault Traffic van just after our first year of trading. It was quite spacious and I installed shelving that enabled stock to stay in their boxes and be easily accessible. We also needed to be able to carry Conduit on the roof and I started to draw up a design for it.

Around the same time, October 2006 one of my mate's Scotty was turning 40. It was a Surprise at a Pub in Sydney. Amanda organised a Hotel and we arrived late afternoon and checked in. I wanted to chill and decided to have a bath. I heard some giggling outside the door but thought it was one of the other Wives going to the Party.

Before you knew it, the door was "flung" open and it wasn't what I thought I was hearing. It was my good mate Tim form England! I almost jumped out of the bath and he was holding a Cricket Bat. Caroline was there and like normal she was laughing, like you have never seen.

Little did I know it had been planned for months and Amanda asked Scotty's Wife Cas if it was ok Tim and Caroline came along.

The reason he was holding a Cricket Bat was he stole it from me one day at my house in the UK. It was homed in Tim and Caroline's downstairs toilet and we both made a "pact", if Tim was to come to Australia one day he must bring the bat with him.

I was still trying to Comprehend what just went on. I changed and we all headed out for Scotty's surprise 40th! On our way to the Venue, like normal Tim, myself and I think Pes went for a beer. We arrived a little late but the Surprise went well and everyone had a good night!

They both stayed at Sally Place and borrowed a spare car from Aussie. They went to the Mountains one day and it was late afternoon and I was out the front when they arrived back. I asked Tim how the car went and like normal he took the piss and said, "yeh it went well, got it up to nearly 200 kilometres!" He has such a funny sense of humour and we laughed like anything on their visit.

When he was there the rack was finished for the top of the van and I asked him if he was ok to come to Aussie and help me install it. I'm glad he came along as he is really good with his hands and we installed it in the morning. He met a new Employee Ryan that day and straight away Tim started banter with him. Ryan was so gullible and Tim pounced on this. That afternoon we headed up the Coast and met Amanda and Caroline and had a good few days away.

After about 2 weeks we were ready to go and it was decided to send out another Employee, John in the Mobile Van as he had a Sales background. It was in general taken ok and the Electricians understood our Concept.

Although John was trying his best, he was not really penetrating enough and I decided to bring him back Internally and I sent out Scott in the Van. We tried sticking to the same areas on the same days to give it continuity. There were only a few times Scott had to head out of area as an Electrician needed something urgently.

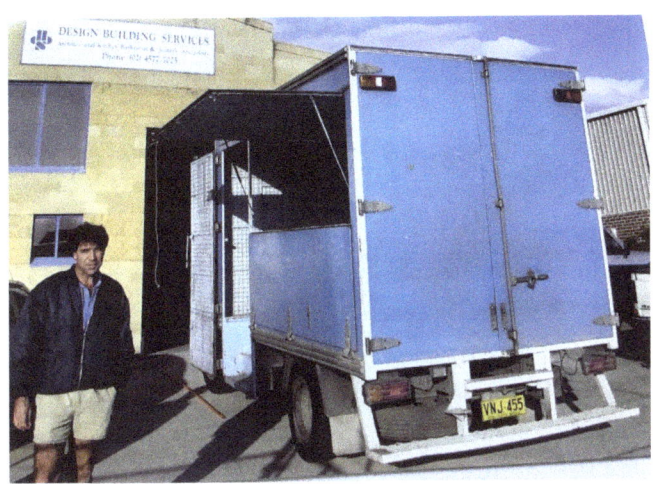

My Longest known mate Ken, from #26 standing next to the Big Truck at his work. He fitted out all the internal shelving. Ken did lots of work for me over the years, he is a Great Tradesman!

Big Truck finished, "Delivering the Trade Counter to You" was our Slogan.

The van was ok but I was always thinking what if the Electrician was able to actually walk in a vehicle and maybe buy more. All Directors agreed to invest in a bigger truck and I hunted a suitable one, albeit and old model. When I bought it off the original owner at Bankstown, he cried and after it was sign written I sent him some photos and he was so pleased.

So we had the Branch at McGraths Hill and two mobile vehicles running around. It was around 2005 that we approached a fella who I knew in the Trade and lived on the Beaches. We wanted to expand over there as I was well aware how disorganised the Sparkies were. I was also confident if we had the correct person with "skin" in the game, it will work.

We all spent a lot of time and money with Nathan and we were just about to engage with Solicitors and he pulled out. I was so disappointed as I trusted him and it was my recommendation that failed! The whole process cost approximately $10,000 to no avail.

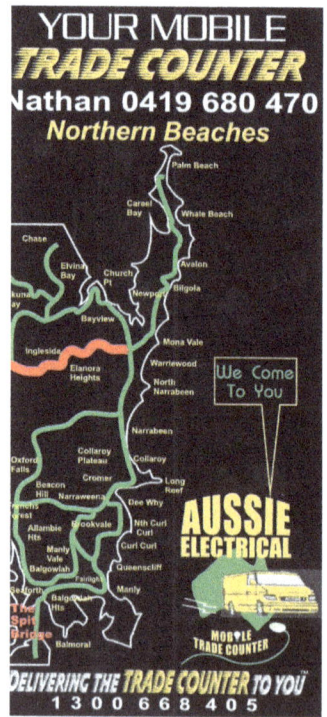

Everything was set up
but to be "Let Down" at the
Last Minute, poor form.

Juan on the BBQ at a Customer ,
he made a few visits from the UK.

COMPETITION:

It was around 2005/06, a local Competitor who I mentioned earlier started to get real traction. For Legal reasons this Competitor will only be referred to as 10%! It was over 12 years later that I was told by a Sparky who had dealt with 10% from the very beginning some disturbing information. The Owner of 10% said to a small group of Electricians, "I will charge you's only 10% on top of my Costs!"

There are a few things in this that are quite disturbing. Having worked for Mutli National Companies in both the UK and Australia, there was always a "line in the sand" of where you need to be to start being profitable. It was always somewhere between 17/20% Gross Profit.

10% was using the "Chinese Mentality", ie they put on a constant % and worked from there. The problem with this approach is "Market Conditions" are never considered! What I mean by this, let me explain.

One of the most common Power Points used in Australia is made by HPM. The "Cost" of an #XL777 back in the early 2000's was approx $5.00. The "Sell Price" for an #XL777 was somewhere between $6.50/7.00 to the Electricians. This means when 10% use the "Chinese Strategy" by putting on only 10% from "Cost", the Power Point's "Sell Price" becomes $5.50! This intern means that 10% all of a sudden have created a "NEW" Market Price. On top of this the local "Big Boys" Years of hard work trying to keep some consistency and make some money has being "Saturated" immediately!

I have only mentioned one example, so try and consider what pressure I was having when this was applied to "ALL" products! When Aussie Electrical moved into the Hawkesbury we were very aware not to take on the two Multi Nationals across the other side of Town on "Price"! We knew if we did, they were large enough to retaliate and really hurt us! We wanted to focus on Service and maintain sensible Pricing. More on 10% later!

Another example of the "Chinese Mentality" is with a Lighting Manufacturer who are in Fact "Chinese Owned". The biggest selling lighting product sold is the Led Downlight. Most Suppliers were hovering around the Post $10 mark and things were running along smoothly for everyone. All of a sudden the Company without mentioning their name were selling them below $10 and in some cases $7.50. All they were doing was whacking on a % and "never" considered or explored what the "Market" price actually was!

So there I was stocking other Manufacture's Led Downlights and the Electricians were not Buying them. The other disturbing thing I found out first hand, this Chinese Company was giving away "Free" stock with large orders. This was a way in not lowering the Cost to such a degree that may have "Crippled" the Industry. 10% was a Big Customer to them and rather than sell the "Free" product for a "Realistic" price they were almost giving it away to the Local Sparkies!

I mentioned earlier we had a Bunnings on our doorstep. We never really considered them as such a big threat back when Aussie Electrical started. I still remember having a conversation with a young Sparky. I asked him where is he buying his cable from? I was expecting one of the Majors close by or 10%. He said, "Bunnings" and it demonstrated to me the mentality with some of them, especially the smaller ones!

Think about this. He parks his van, walks a good 20/30 metres to the entrance, grabs a trolley, walks another 40/50 metres to the Electrical Isle. Once he arrives there, he has to load the cable on the trolley "himself" and that's only if there is enough cable. He walks back to the Checkout, pays for it on a Credit Card and walks back to his van, unloads the Cable and walks another 20 metres to return the trolley and another 20 metres back to his van.

Now surely it's a lot easier to park his Van just outside Aussie Electrical and ask for his cable at the Counter. One of our Staff picks it up and puts it on the trolley and wheels it out to the van for him? Don't forget he has not paid for it unlike at Bunnings as he has an Account with us and normally has a min 30 Days to pay for it. Our Staff helps load it in his van and brings the trolley back.

My last "Two" paragraphs are so significant to try and understand the pressure I was under. If the Electrician can not appreciate "Service" and only focus on "Price", what Future did we have.

NEW IDEA: #3- ON SITE SHOP.

It wasn't long after our rejection for the Beaches, the Rouse Hill Project was gathering momentum. I was given another contact with the main Lend Lease person who was responsible for the Project. His name was Trevor Battle and I communicated with him over a 12 month period. Within that time I went out in the bigger truck to see if the Sparkies liked the idea of a Mobile Concept in a larger vehicle.

Yes, when I met the Sparkies they were more than happy to walk in the Truck and we're very impressed with the idea. We did open up some new Accounts and they also Phoned through to the Branch for gear. I still however wasn't happy with the "On Road" Phone Calls to the Mobile Truck and I started to accept maybe the Concept was not viable?

All was not lost as we had a Truck ideally suitable to take to the Rouse Hill Site and leave there. I was recontacted by Lend Lease and arranged a meeting with Trevor Battle on site. The meeting was mid morning and Scott arrived with the Truck in the car park. When he got out he said, "it had been playing up" and he tried to restart it. It did not start and it was a good 50 metres away from the Site Office!

I thought to myself, we have been "communicating" with Lend Lease for "2 ½ YEARS" and at the final hurdle we may stuff it up if he asks me to drive it over! Luckily he didn't and we both walked over to the Truck. I opened the side shelter and doors and he walked up the stairs first. We both stood at the counter looking out and I nervously asked him, "what do you think" and I'll never forget his response; "This will work"! I tapped him on the shoulder and said, "Thanks, Let's Go"!

We were given an area right next door to the Site Entrance. We bought a large Shipping Container to help store the bulkier goods. I put Ryan in the Truck On Site and I was ferrying gear from our Branch which was only a 15minute drive. There was one day I was in the truck and a Kiwi guy made a visit. I asked him what Trade was he and he replied, "I'm a Sparky and are doing the 3 Residential Towers". My reply was, "we need to get to know you mate" and he said, "good luck trying to deal with my Owner"! His name was Ness and he gave me a name who was the next one down from the Boss.

I met a guy named Peter and soon into the conversation he too said, "the Boss is a hard bloke to do business with!" In the back of my mind, I thought bring it on as I have dealt with lots of hard arses in the UK! I eventually met the Owner one morning and he got out of his "flash" Ute and seemed very standoffish. Within 60 seconds he said, "don't ever try ripping me Fucking off"! I replied with, "I can do business with you!" His name was Sean.

Around this time I met one of the Fathers from Daisy's soccer. I asked him what he did for a living and he was in the Home Theatre Industry. I never thought any more about it and it was a few weeks later he made a visit to the Rouse Hill Site. His name was Charlie and expressed interest in getting into the Electrical Industry.

I had Employed a guy named Ken about 12/18 months previously as I was feeling stretched hunting New Business and overseeing the Rouse Hill Shop. He was to look after the Branch for me. Unfortunately that's all he did and although he had a lot of Experience, he didn't really bring along any New Business.

This was a normal observation I made in my time working in Australia in the Electrical Wholesale Industry. So many of the Managers came up from in some cases, Driver, Stores, Trade Sales, Assistant Manager and Manager. The majority of them had not done any External Sales chasing New Business. Ken was in this Category and so too was Allan who came and worked for me for about 6 months and he too didn't bring any New Business and he was previously a Regional Manager for one of the Big Boys!

This is why I tried getting another Director in the Business with "Skin" in the Game and help take away the load that was building up on me. Yes I took it on board at the start with 3 Silent Partners but as the years rolled on it was obvious to me I was "flogging" myself. I never really had the chance to take any holidays in those early days and I knew within myself it was taking its Toll on me!

An Aerial shot of the New Rouse Hill Town Centre. We were located near the Red Arrow for over 12 Months. No other Competitor had tried such a thing!

I took Charlie on as the Rouse Hill Site was getting busier and I knew he had the People Skills to fit in and do whatever was required. It was not long after Charlie started and Ken put in his Notice. He did not let on but soon I learnt he joined a Cheap Importer of Electrical gear, located half way between the Branch and the Rouse Hill Site. He approached a lot of my Customers and a few bought from him which was disappointing.

The "On Site" Concept worked really well and definitely got Business that we never had. I was still dealing with the Electrical Company who did the 3 Residential Towers a good 10 plus years later. Lend Lease were really good and never once asked me for any money.

Our On Site Shop at Rouse Hill.

BUYING GROUP:

In the middle of 2008 we approached an Electrical Wholesale Buying Group with the recommendation by Skewsy from Clipsal. We wanted to wait 5 years before applying as we were in a better Trading position and I was able to Commit time to the Group. I met up with one of the Directors, Greg at our Branch. He was impressed with our set up and the last thing was to send our Financials for final approval.

We were accepted and I went to a meeting not long after. They were all very welcoming and although a little nervous, I slowly settled in. There was a trip to Perth in the next few weeks and I was invited to come, although only a new member.

There were lots of good guys and one in particular I connected with straight away, Jason (Judy). He was from the Country Town of Orange and although he wasn't into Cricket we just clicked. He wasn't "out there" like me, really Laid Back! I met his Uncle one day at my Branch and you can see why he is such a Top bloke!

There was another guy who was one of the "Founding" Members, John (JC). Although a good 10 years older than myself, I think he found me a bit of a "Battler"! I listened to him as much as possible as he and his Business Partner Martyn had over 30 years of Experience and had over 30 stores. Little did I know that our Friendship was genuine and has lasted for nearly 15 years!

Aussie started to slowly reap the rewards of being in the Buying Group by way of Rebates paid due to purchases from our Suppliers. On average we were receiving a Min 60k a year and it helped pay many Expenses.

Our 1st Family Holiday with the Buying Group was Fiji. We stayed at a great Hotel which had a massive pool. Henry and Daisy had so much fun swimming and interacting with the other kids in the Group.

There was an interesting moment when Amanda and the kids went out with most of the other Mums for an Island Tour. Whilst they were out, there was a Tsunami Warning! I was with all the other Owners in a large Conference Room and we had to be on guard. We were unable to contact the Girls but I thought they were in a safer place in a bus as they'd find higher ground. All was well and the threat was lowered but a real reminder how quick things can happen.

Our 2nd Holiday with the Group was Hawaii. We stayed right on Waikiki in a Hotel that was one of the originals built on the Beach. Once again the kids had a ball, swimming in the Ocean and some-times with the large Turtles. We stayed on after the Buying Group left and really chilled out which I needed. We made a visit to Pearl Harbour and although the kids were quite young it was a surreal experience! Anyway back to the Buying Group later.

UK SURPRISE:

In about May of 2009 Amanda and I received an Invitation to Hattie and Luey's combined 18th and 21st in the UK. We put the invite on the fridge and I kept saying to myself, I'd love to go! The June long weekend was coming up and on the Thursday morning before, I said to Charlie at work, "I'd love to go to the party". He replied with, "why don't you go, I can look after the Branch." I called Amanda saying, "I'd like to go to the Party" she said, "what Party?" I responded with "Hattie and Luey's". There was a pause and she replied with" ok why not!"

I booked a flight straight away and on the Friday morning headed for the Airport. At the Bus Stop just up the road I texted my Cousins to let them know I'd be away for about 10 days and thought all was ok?

I arrived at Heathrow early on the Saturday morning and caught a

Bus to Reading. I jumped off the Bus and caught a Black Cab to Keith and Margaret's home. It drove into their front parking area and I got out. Keith was there and like always took it in his stride when seeing me. I said, "Gday I'm here for Hattie and Luey's Party". He replied with, "are Amanda and the kids with you?" It was then I spotted Margaret looking out of the kitchen window. After having a sleep and shower, I headed to the Cricket Club to kill a bit of time. I caught up with a few guys and watched the 1st Team play and had a couple of Pints.

I headed back to Amanda's Parents home and got changed. It was a Beach theme and I brought over a snorkel with me as I wanted to be slightly camouflaged. I drove Keith's car over to Tim and Caroline's in Tadley where the Party was. It was just around the corner where I stopped to get myself sorted. There was a 2 minute drive and I was wearing the snorkel and goggles. I drove just past their drive and parked the car as I didn't want anyone to see me.

I walked into their front yard with my video camera on and walked around the side towards the back. I spotted Caroline straight away and headed in her direction. She looked at me trying to work out who I was and in a second or two she said, "Fuck, Fuck, no Way!" She was in hysterics and I spotted Tim standing and chatting to a few people having a beer. I walked towards him and no doubt he heard Caroline and worked out it was me and turned around and just laughed. I said to him, "I wanted to re pay his Surprise he made on me a few years earlier with the Cricket Bat!" I gave Hattie and Luey a big hug and had a great night, although very Jet-lagged!

The following Sat I played a game for Boyne Hill in their 3rd Team. It was great fun putting the pads on for one last game. As I was batting a few of the guys I played with were heckling me on the Boundary.

There was a Club Event in the evening and I had a few beers with the boys! After, I went back to Chumbly's with Willy and had more beers and talked about the Old Days. They are both Top Blokes; Chumbly is your typical English well spoken Old Chap and Willy loves Expanding his stories but is extremely Loyal.

Two great mates! Willy and Chumbly.

When I returned back to Australia we had a "Link Up" Directors meeting at my Cousin's Office. Straight away my Cousins brought up that they were unhappy that I left the Business without any notice. It was a real shock to me as I was confident Charlie was more than capable in looking after the Branch whilst I was away. It was at that meeting, I felt things had shifted and was a real sign that they were not happy where Aussie Electrical was at!

It was then I noticed that things were starting to take their toll with me "Mentally!" There are lots of opinions about going into Business with Family and Friends. That's easy for others to say, however when they were the "only" people available, I was willing to take that risk. It also reaffirmed why I was so keen to get someone like Chappo on board as he was not Family.

PROMOTIONAL DAYS:

Around 2009/10 things were really tough so I wanted to do something to really let the Local Sparkies and Tradies know we were still around. I knew a local businessman who had a side business flying helicopters. I asked him about an idea of picking up people on the vacant land next door and do a lap around the area. He had a look at the site and said "no worries."

Once again we got the Radio Show to come and do a Live Gig with Robbo and the boys. We also invited some of our Suppliers to come along and meet the Sparkies. So there I am looking up in the sky and I spotted the Helicopter coming our way. I kept it a Surprise but arranged our Logo to be stuck on both sides of the Chopper.

The Vacant Land opposite was the Landing Area and I cleaned it up as best as possible on my own over two weekends. When the Chopper Landed it was such a "relief" as so much work had gone on in the background.

From memory there were about 15/20 trips made with 4 at a time. The Pilot had to contact the RAAF Base close by as he was in their airspace. I gave out heaps of tee shirts with our logo on the back. There were a few "dong dongs" on the Road outside as drivers were so absorbed by the Chopper taking off and landing, they were not watching who was in front of them.

There was a funny moment when my Dad came up to me a said, "under no circumstances you, Amanda and the Kids go in that Helicopter"! He asked, "where are they" and I pointed up in the Sky! The Tradies talked about that day for years and I was really hoping that New Business may have come from it?

We did lots of things over the years for our Customers but I later found out 10% was heavily into Entertaining and did it on a more regular basis. It takes it toll always Wining and Dining Customers and I wasn't prepared to let it affect my home life in any way! No doubt this was another reason I found it hard to "prise away" any of the Sparkies that were dealing with 10%.

Chopper coming in to land on the vacant property opposite. This was when we changed our Logo trying to make it more Modern and attract all Trades.

Taking off for another lap, what a Day!

*Gavin Robertson (Robo) and Graeme Hughes doing
a Live Broadcast on Chopper Day.*

Chopper Day with the Radio, notice our 3 key Messages on the Banner!

BUSINESS: TAKES IT'S TOLL.

Pom was the first person who showed signs of wanting out in Aussie
Electrical. Things were becoming tense between him and my Cousins
as well as Juan. He was upfront that he wasn't prepared to put any

more money into the Business. He was also concerned about the long term viability for the Business. He was paid out from memory $50,000 but definitely lost money as an Investor. My Cousins and Juan hung around for about 12 months and they too wanted out.

Although we were loosing money each year, I still had faith in the Business and wasn't prepared to give it up that easily! I fort too hard getting it to where is was, let alone worked my guts out, so I borrowed more money to pay them out.

Sales over the Years. As you can see we "Hovered" between $1Mil-$1.2Mil in the last five Years. I was slowly "Sinking" and Searching for a "Good" Customer to help "Turn" things around!

07/08 $2,234,672 Rouse Hill Shop
08/09 $1,944,228 Top Ryde Shop
09/10 $1,254,090
10/11 $1,235,480
11/12 $1,368,840 New Branch
12/13 $1,075,089
13/14 $1,216,915
14/15 $1,286,517
15/16 $1,122,600
16/17 $1,062,282
17/18 $1,024,240

Not long after, my Cousins changed their Electrician and although they were no longer Owners in the Business, they made it clear that the material needed to be purchased form Aussie Electrical. Unfortunately he too never stuck to the Deal.

So, I was totally on my own and that didn't worry me. I was however aware of my own Financial position and knew I had no one else to go to for money as in the past. Going through anyone leaving a Business is extremely stressful and I went through it twice over a 2 year period. A few years before, I went to my Doctor to let him know I was not coping well Mentally. He referred me to a Phycologist and as a result it was thought best to go on Medication. It was a bit of a shock but did explain how sometimes I got emotional when the heat was on in some of those Directors Meetings.

I also found when I was in bed I'd have aches going through my arms and legs. On top of that, if there was a lot going on at work my mind never really relaxed. The treatment helped in both areas, although a good Ten years later I am still on Medication.

It's interesting how everyone is wired differently and on the surface someone may appear to be in control. I recall my Aunty saying to me that I was a "stress head" and I revisited her comment and said, "No, I am a Carer".

I was very aware that I was putting adverse pressure on myself, especially with the New Ideas but I really thought there needed to be something else outside the normal Electrical Wholesaler. As an Example one of the Members in the Buying Group had a Telstra Shop next door to his Branch and also had a Makita Shop within his Store. Maybe being in a Country Town enabled him to take on new things with more confidence as the Competition was not as great?

After the Rouse Hill Project finished there was another Site in Top Ryde and Lend Lease once again allowed me to be set up for a good twelve months. I put a guy called Darryl at Top Ryde in the Mobile Truck. He was so Loyal and was happy to start early for the Tradies. I was getting to the Site early and selling Safety Vests, Boots, Glasses, Hard Hats etc in the Induction Room with Darryl downstairs in the Mobile Truck selling to the Sparkies and Tradies. Lend Lease needed the Tradies to be identified easily so a Pink Vest was chosen.

There was an interesting situation early one morning and a guy somehow came into the Induction Room before it opened. I was setting up and he asked for a Hard Hat. I got one out of my Storage Cage that we built and he asked me "how much?" I said, "20 Bucks" and he reluctantly gave me a $20 note. As I was just about to hand the "Hard Hat" to him he said, "your Ripping us Off!" I still had the $20 in one hand and reached over and handed it back and said to him, "Fuck Off and go to Bunnings and get one!" Once again another classic example of a Customer not appreciating "Service" and only "Price!"

Once I finished at Top Ryde I headed back to the Branch and do whatever needed to be done. I was feeling the work load taking its toll but I knew deep down the Top Ryde Site was only going to be a twelve month situation and had to make "Hay whilst the Sun was Shining"!

Our Cash Flow was really good due to Top Ryde, however like anything there has to be a finish. Unfortunately there was not a Third Site although, I did approach Bangeroo in the City. I put my Truck up for Sale and it was so sad seeing her on top of the Tow Truck driving away.

When you are on the Roller Coaster, it's only when you get off that you really understand what you have put your body through. Both Rouse Hill and Top Ryde required lots of Self Belief and I am sure there were knockers out there who didn't think we were able to follow it through.

There was another extremely stressful period when we relocated the Branch from the back of the Industrial Estate to the front. I knew the owner in Unit 1 from my Electrical Tech days. His business didn't require Road Frontage and it was agreed that he re-locates to my Unit#8. Back to this later.

NEW IDEA: #4- RECYCLE LAMPS AND TUBES.

I was doing Business with Sydney Flemington Markets and it was at a meeting when they brought up the problem of getting rid of their Lamps in a Safe way. I said, "we can do that" and they asked me to come back with some pricing etc. I thought, this is my time to have Business outside of the Main Electrical Stream.

We had to move quickly to show the Markets we were capable in fixing their problem. Charlie did all the Marketing and Research and we came up with the name Recycle Light. We were basically the middle man and collected the Lamps and Tubes and when we had too many, we sent them to be Recycled. We charged about $1.00 per Tube and provided documentation that they were being Recycled Legally.

We also made a good contact at CBA Bank in Olympic Park and they too had issues with getting rid of their Lamps and Tubes. We came up with a Trolley Solution with small areas to house both new and old lamps as the Tradesman pushed it around the office. There was even an area to hold a small ladder.

Charlie and I also introduced Recycle Light to the Buying Group as it was not foreign for Members to do their own Presentations. They were quite ok with the Concept but I wasn't hearing any real enthusiasm and it became obvious it was more important to Us than Them!

Our biggest obstacle was there was no "Legislation" enforced in Australia, so therefore it was "not" Illegal to "dump" Fluorescent Tubes. In Europe and America it is "Illegal" to "dump" Fluorescent Lamps and Tubes!

Ok, it may not have been Illegal but most of the bigger Corporates did not want any bad Press on their Environmental practises. I witnessed 1st hand with one of the Two Major Supermarkets that they were literally dumping Fluorescent Tubes into a big Waste Disposable Bin!

Fluorescent Tubes contain Mercury and when smashed the small amount of Mercury is exposed to the elements. This is why we never went down the route to actually Recycle the Tubes as it is an extremely dangerous process. Due to the Ignorance and without Legislation, Recycle Light only ticked along over the years which was another disappointment.

We showed off Recycle Light at the Chopper Day.
Notice the Trolley in the Background.

NEW IDEA: #5- HEATING PANELS

I got an Email from Pommy who was living in the UK regarding a new opportunity. His Brother had a contact with a Company who were selling Heating Panels in Europe. They were interested in finding a Distributor in Australia. I looked into it and had no idea what Infra Red Heating was but was keen to know.

European Technology gave me confidence with the quality rather then cheap Chinese Rubbish. The panels were quite good in appearance and were able to be installed on the ceiling, walls, as well as on a stand.

My main interest once again was to try and have something that was not easily "Shopped" on Price unlike the Electrical Wholesale game. I also wanted to be the "Sole" Importer so I had total control in Sales and Marketing.

I trialled them myself and I was really impressed with their performance and how they looked. The big thing about the German Technology was how "efficient" they were compared to others similar. The Brand Name was I think a bit "Corny" being Sunnyheat but I was to be appointed the Australian Distributorship.

There was a lot of time invested into it and Yes some may think reading this Book, I took my eye of the ball with the Wholesaling Business. Far from it, I just worked harder! I took Sunnyheat to the Sydney Exhibition Centre and it went from the Friday to Sunday. From memory it cost approximately $4000 but I really thought we needed to be visible. It was in late May but unfortunately it was not Winter and although people understood the Technology, I didn't really have the take up as I was hoping.

I went out to visit lots of Architects and Energy Efficient Companies and although they liked the new Technology they were not really rushing to Specify it. I did make a Cold Call to one of the large Project Homes Selection Centres and immediately was welcomed. I installed the Heating Panel samples in their Gallery and had one Sign Written as a Joint Venture.

I was also keen to explore the idea of having them installed in Outside Entertaining. I ordered three 1500x300 panels and installed them into my Alfresco Area at our home in Sally Place. I Invited the Main person of the Gallery to my home one Evening. I arranged a few nibbles and drinks as well as I invited my Cousin Richard as he was very good in the Marketing area and a Builder. Unfortunately the Main guy Alan was only to stay for about max 20 minutes as he doubled booked and was on his way to the Movies. Just another example of how you go all out and someone can be so Ignorant as to not understanding how important to me the meeting was!

The Excuse that came back not going ahead was the main builder Eden Brae was concerned if the Customer was walking around one of their Display Homes in Winter and walked outside to the Alfresco and noticed the warmth from the Panels it may distract them from concentrating on the Home itself. What a load of Bullshit!

I took out the Panels from the Gallery and Targeted the Bikram Indoor Yoga Studios. What I found out was in Sydney the Climate was warmer then in Melbourne and I was approached by a Company who took interest in requiring Sunnyheat.

As much as it felt like another "Failed Adventure", I did a deal with them and let Sunnyheat go. We installed multiple Panels in Sally Place and enjoyed the constant heat and lower Electricity Bills.

Heating Panel specially made for Eden Brae Homes selection centre.

NEW IDEA: #6–BRANCH MOVE

It got to the stage that we really needed to consider moving down the front for better Exposure. The Local Sparkies were not really supporting us, so I was hoping anyone outside the Area may spot us as they drove past and pop in. Suzanne and Charlie tried to talk me out of it but I said, "it was more "Catastrophic" if we stayed at the back!"

As I mentioned earlier I knew the owner of Unit #1, Michael. He was well known as a hoarder of anything from Car Parts to Electrical Tools. On top of this, he was a "Steady Eddie" and did everything at his pace. I kept on asking him when was he ready and his response was a standard, Soon!

We were well prepared at our end with all our racking wrapped and wheels added so we were able to literally roll them down the driveway. We finally started the move and it was obvious he wasn't ready and the Stress levels went up for him and myself! Ken from #26 Charles St made a visit as he knew I was moving. He stood in Unit #1 and said, "you need help!" He went away and came back with his truck and a few boys. They started loading all the stuff on the back of his truck.

It was so stressful, the owner of Unit #1 almost pulled out of the move. He just struggled with everybody else helping out as he wanted to be in control. Without exaggerating, I reckon there were a min 20 trips, thanks Ken! By moving down the front it added an extra $20,000 per year in Rent and I was hoping the gamble was worth it?

Account #30's offered to do all the Electrical changes as I literally didn't have the time and energy to do it myself. Taking up his offer for doing the work Free was really appreciated. We finally got in and although it took a few weeks to settle in properly, fortunately we were attracting more Visitors.

NEW IDEA: #7- CHRISTMAS SHOP.

We sold Christmas Lights in Unit#8 mainly to our existing Customers but only in small quantities. I was keen to see if we were able to ramp up the Sales with an actual Shop in the new location. I was lucky to find a Supplier who sold Quality as I didn't need the hassle with returns. We revamped our Office upstairs and Suzanne and Leisa made it into a nice Christmas Shop. We did $50,000 in Sales in our 1st Year and that gave me confidence to keep it going.

In our 2nd Year my Brother Justin, generously paid for and built an

Extension to the Christmas Shop. It was a long room, at least 25mts by 5mts wide. This enabled us to really create a fantastic Experience for the Shoppers and especially the Kids. I also "lit" up the front garden as well on our building and at night cars stopped to have a look. We did $45,000 in Sales in the 2nd Year, down $5000 but I was still Positive about Year 3.

Come Year 3, a really good mate who I met previously through Customer#30's, Mark was a Carpenter. Jonson as I call him, built another room in the Christmas Shop and we called it the Christmas Cave. I will talk about Jonson later.

In Year 3, unfortunately our Sales fell to $25,000 which I felt unfair. I even got dressed up as Santa Claus for the kids and waving to the passing traffic. There was more Competition with Bunnings as well as Online and a few Christmas Shops started to pop up. On top of this, our returns were very low and maybe we were too Expensive as we wanted to sell Quality as I've already mentioned.

My main reason for the Christmas Shop was to attract New Customers to Aussie Electrical and hoping that they may come back throughout the year. Yes, I did notice some follow through but I closed the Shop after Year 4 as Sales dropped to only $12,500.

Christmas Shop in Revamped Office Upstairs. Sales went from $50,000 to $12,500 over 4 Years!

The Long Room that Justin built, so many Kids had Fantastic Memories!

BUYING GROUP- VIETNAM

It was Sept 2013 and we had a Conference in HO Chi Minh, Vietnam. I went on my own as I wasn't in the Financial position to bring the whole Family like in the past. The first thing I noticed heading to our Hotel was all the Motorbikes. There were hundreds and hundreds of them and there were not too many rules being applied. Our Hotel was in the middle of the City and we went for a walk and visited a few Bars.

One of our Day Trips was to the Tunnels where the Vietnamese hid and fought the Enemy in the Vietnam War. Our guide showed us how deadly "Booby Traps" were used and they were quite frightening. The thought of one of our Aussie or USA soldiers falling victim to one of these made your body cringe!

We went in a small section of one of the Tunnels used in the Conflict and let me tell you they were only just big enough to get a standard body through. Hearing how they used and constructed the Tunnels as well as the area they covered was bewildering. A moment to savour was getting the opportunity to use an actual Machine Gun used in the War. The Power was unforgettable and all of us kept talking about it after.

Every Trip there was always a night dedicated for the Suppliers and the Buying Group to enjoy. We all went to the Hard Rock Café and it started like normal with Dinner and everyone relaxed. One of the boys arranged for beers to come out with something I've never seen before. It was a Tube set up with Ice surrounding the glass as well as a handle to stop and start the flow of beer. As soon as I spotted it, I knew there may be trouble ahead!

I was on a "high" with my 10th Birthday and the atmosphere was Building. Everyone was getting on it and I somehow I had this massive gadget in my possession. I was walking around the dance floor and pouring beer down people's throats as they where dancing. Even some of the older Members were getting into it and everyone was having a blast.

Here we go, I was so, so "revved" up, I decided to "Strip" down and start dancing on the Stage. There I was totally "Naked" and all the Boys were encouraging me on. I am not sure exactly how long it went on for but I do remember one of the Directors Greg, coming up and "hooking" me off the Stage. It was quite late and most of the Families had left but I immediately knew I was in trouble!

The next day we had our normal one on ones with our Suppliers and when I arrived at the Conference Room a few of the Directors took me to one side. I listened to how disappointed they were and how I let the reputation of the Buying Group down. I think it was my good mate Jonny, JC who suggested that I apologised to the Members and Suppliers.

I agreed and I was asked to speak and given a Microphone. It was one of the hardest things I've ever done. I explained it was Aussie Electrical's 10th Birthday and the emotions just took over. I said, "I am so sorry that I have let you all down". That's as much as I can remember and I went to a Coffee Shop to reflect on what I had just been through!

I never let Amanda know until we all got back together at the Group's Christmas party in the City a few months later. She was annoyed I told her on the night rather then when I got back but to be honest I was embarrassed!

UK VISIT-AMANDA'S 50TH

Late December 2014 we all went away for Amanda's 50th Birthday. We planned the trip to arrive a few days before the 24th, being Amanda's big day. On her Birthday we went to a local Pub and all Celebrated her turning 50. The next day we had Christmas at their house and it was good just sitting around eating and drinking.

Early in the new year 2015, we had a big day at the Cricket Club. It was 25 years since we Won the League and 125 Years since the Club was Founded. It was great spending quality time with everyone and reminiscing about the good old days. Boycee he was unable to attend as he was skiing in Europe. I was disappointed as I wanted to catch up with him for a beer. His wife Marlene came along and passed on Boycee's disappointment with not being able to come.

We were all drinking away and all of a sudden there was a knock on the Club's glass doors. Someone opened the curtains and doors and this bloke walks in wearing ski goggles dressed up in ski gear and holding skis. It was bloody Boycee and I just cracked up and gave him a big hug. He always was doing stuff like this and that's why everyone loves him as he makes people laugh!

Boycee, Surprising me at our Cricket Reunion.

I was asked to say some words and I acknowledged the Achievements made whilst I was there from '1990-1997', here are a few.

-Colts Day
-Bonfire Night
-Champions 1990
-Runners Up 1994
-Boundary Hedge
-Club New Entry Drive
-Ashes Tour 94/95

I also reflected on a few of the Members who had passed and were close to me.

-Nikky Watson
-Mike King
-Derek Fitzgibbon

Some of the Championship Team in 1990! Willy, Shawy, Kingy, Crocko, Chumbly, Palfs, Suhail, Myself, Eileen- Scorer.

It was great to be back with some of the guys who played in the Championship Team. It really reinforced how Cricket has shaped my Life to which I am so appreciative of.

Suhail, was dynamic when batting, able to hit a 6 over Square Leg from Off Stump!

Willy, had a Great Eye, had the ability to hit a Straight 6 Off any Bowler!

Crocko was quite quick, I remember his spell against Keith Arthurton, it was a Rippa!

Chumbly, was your typical English "Old Fashion" Cricketer, takes his time!

Shawy, a true Competitor, always wanted to Bowl or Bat, top notch Player!

Palfs, was extremely Gutsy, Calm, Competitive, Good Bloke all rolled into One!

Kingy took a young Side to believe in Themselves, a Good Mentor and Captain!

I also had a few beers with my mate Palfs at the Reunion and at a Pub a few weeks later. Little did I know it was the last time I was to be with him as he passed away a few years back with Lung Cancer. He was our Captain when we were Runners Up in 1994!

Whilst we were in England, Willy took myself and Henry to watch Chelsea play at Stanford Bridge. It's such an Iconic ground and the Supporters Shop is Massive. Henry had a great time and will hold onto this memory for a long time.

CUSTOMERS, HARD WORK!

A moment which was disappointing was I made a phone call back to Aussie Electrical. I still recall hanging out Amanda's Mum's window in the "frost" trying to get Reception. I had recently done a deal with a Medium size Contractor who were doing a large project. I made it very clear I was going to be away in the UK and we were very short staffed. True to form, he put lots of pressure on my staff and totally ignored my discussion that I was going to be away!

I lasted just over 12 months dealing with him! He is the most "horrible" person I have sold to in over 30 Years. I asked him one day, "how do you value Electrical Wholesalers?" He did not answer and just carried on with his Bullshit.

I made mention earlier of my Cousin's Electrician and I was hoping that he gave Aussie the Support we needed. It was after the Christmas break and I went to his Factory for what I thought a normal visit. As usual I went to the Dock Gates and blocking the Entry was a whole "Pallet" of material. It was from one of my Competitors, JR Turk!

He wasn't in, so I called him straight away. When he answered I asked him,"how much in % do my Cousins give you against your Turnover?" He replied with 75%, not knowing my Motive to the Question. I said, "why the Fuck am I only getting 15% of it?" I was so pissed off and Yes at the beginning my Cousins didn't want any issues, however looking back we made a big mistake not to sort it. Remember I didn't have any real Bankers as I mentioned working in the Beaches and the UK, I or WE needed that Business!

Some may be reading this and be taken back but I seem to attract awkward Customers. I mentioned before about a Company who I was recommended. We "gave" him a large Construction Site as my Cousins were doing the job. We thought if we give him the job, Aussie Electrical will benefit with the Material. Sounds a deal yeh, however I had to sit him down one day and explain, "if it was not for me, you didn't have a chance of getting it". He was convinced he won it on Merit. The material on the job was worth approximately 400/450k and we were lucky to get 100/125k. It made my blood boil as the Business needed the revenue and he just disregarded the relationship!

It all came to a "head" one day when Leisa called him asking for Payment. As he was late, Leisa indicated if he wanted to pay by Credit Card there will be a % Charge. He said to Leisa, "tell Nick don't take from the hand that feeds him!" This was after the Large Project had finished and he was only doing small amounts with us. I walked outside and called him and before he had a chance to talk I said, "Listen to exactly what I'm going to say to you! Don't you ever, ever call or visit Aussie Electrical again!, We gave you a Job worth over $1Million and you only gave us over $100 Thousand!" He hung up on me and I never heard from the Grub again.

Roll on nearly 10 Years and he Sold the Business to a really good Fella who started doing Business with Aussie. In the Deal it was "clear" that he was not allowed to contact any of the Customers. Yes, you bet, he totally disregarded this and made contact with them. The matter went Legal and it just shows how "Grubs" like this, think they can do what ever they bloody well like!

Talking about Relationships the next one is my Biggest "Emotional" disappointment. Account #30s as I have mentioned previously came to Aussie Electrical and we started doing business. For the first few years things were going along fine and although I notice a bit of "attitude" I just accepted it. Yes, ok we seemed to get every order, however soon I noticed a change in him. It was when he bought a House that was a stretch too far Financially.

There were several occasions I had to ask him about payment. The response was let's say Flippant and he really started to be a Smart Arse! I love "Banter" and engage big time into it, however when someone starts to be a Smart Arse, I can not "Hack" it!

The thing I noticed about him was he had a "Jekyll and Hyde" Personality! He sucked up to his Customer's and treated me and sometimes my Staff with little or no Respect! I know that he went through a min of 6 Apprentices in the space of 9/12 months. This in itself is Disturbing and I can only feel for the Young Fellas who were treated as Nobodies!

The biggest mistake I made was I took him on as a friend and a customer. When we went out the way he spoke to his wife in a Smart Arse way was appalling! In the end I had to ask him to "try someone else" as I wanted him to see how much we looked after him. At that stage he owed me $55,000 and he fundamentally was using me as a Bank, Interest Free! I had to increase my Overdraft to Support him at 9/10% Interest!

I am a true believer that every "dog" has its day and the Customers I have mentioned that were "hard work" or just generally "Dickheads" will one day get their "up and commons!"

PHILLIP HUGHES: NECK GUARD

I was at work late November 2014 and a Customer informed me that a Cricketer had been hit on the head at the SCG. The gravity of the Incident increased quickly and News came out the Batsman was Phillip Hughes! He sadly passed away a few days later and a large portion of the Community and especially Cricket Lovers were in Mourning.

PHILLIP HUGHES
30 Nov 1988 – 27 Nov 2014

It was late Jan, early Feb, just after the November tragedy and I was reading the Sunday paper. There was almost an identical situation at a 1st Grade game that was played at Mark Taylor Oval in Hornsby. Luckily this time the batsman was able to recover but it was the real Catalyst of me to react! I grabbed Henry's helmet and took it to my Neighbour Danny as he was in the Plastic Moulding Industry. I explained the Article I had just read and asked if he was able to help? He said, "I'll come back with a design".

Within a few days Danny came back with a "Prototype" Neck Guard. It was "see through" and wrapped around Henry's Helmet and I was really impressed with it. I continued with the idea and decided to go all the way and take it to Market. The name was an easy one, HENZ. It is Henry's Nic Name and I thought it was a bit different and adds to the story.

I approached my good mate Spotty and showed him the Prototype. I asked him if he was interested in coming in 50/50 and he said, "Yes!" For the next few months it was backwards and forwards from the Tool Maker and a Design was locked in. We paid for a 3D model as we needed something to show the Sports Industry.

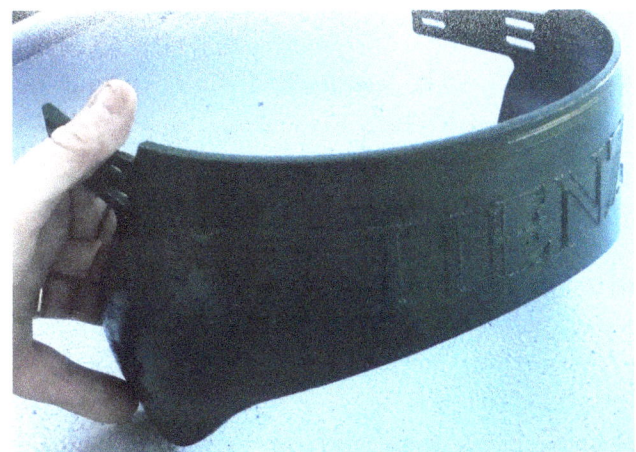

One of our very first 3D Model of HENZ.

My mate Scotty had a good relationship with the Owner of Kingsgrove Sports, Harry Solomons. They are the most recognised Cricket Outlet in the Country and I took the 3D model into show him with Scotty. I pulled it out of my bag and I said to Harry, "it's only "conceptional" and quite Fragile. Harry was looking at it and put force on the ear section and it "snapped" off! He said, "mate, I hope it's stronger than this?" He quite liked the idea, although it was such a new area of protection and so raw since the Incident. I explained why we called it HENZ and he liked the connection with my Son.

We decided to have the Mould made in China as it was a lot cheaper and the Tool Maker had a very good Company that he had dealt with for Years. Yes it went against all my "Morals" but we were not in a financial position to have it made in Australia. From memory it cost approximately $24,000 rather then $40,000 made here.

Yes, we were in the position to have the Neck Guards made in

China but I wanted Danny to Manufacturer them as he came up with the original model. We were also keen to have "Australian Made" to help with Sales both here and Internationally.

Packaging, Marketing and a Safety Report was the three main areas needed doing. We set up a Web Site and had a Photo Shoot at a local Park with Henry and a few mates. It was great fun and the photos were fantastic. The Safety was an area we needed to get right and we approached an Associate Professor at Sydney University who was involved in this Space. We set up a Helmet with HENZ attached and started hitting it from a Bowling Machine approximately 10 metres away.

There were lots of Measurements taken at different speeds (up to 150k's) and the Grill on the helmet broke without the Neck Guard breaking. It was great news that we knew it was Safe to use and a Safety Report was made up.

The mould finally arrived in Sydney and Danny organised to have it transported to the Company he was working for. He hit the button and ran off approximately 1500 in three colours, Navy, Green and Maroon. It was so exciting seeing them 1st Hand but still we had lots to do.

Although Kingsgrove Sports were on Board and we were so "Grateful" for, we needed to get the Brand out there. Spotty had a contact with a Marketing Guru who had lots to do with the Signage on Grounds in India. We arranged a meeting with Neil Maxwell in North Sydney.

After showing him HENZ both attached and non attached to a helmet he said, "you don't have to sell me the Product, I'm happy with it, you need to Shake a few trees!" He picked up his Mobile and called a Reporter for the Sunday Telegraph, Ben Horne. Spotty and I left the meeting both feeling positive and intrigued all in one!

We met up with Ben a few times to discuss a range of things. The main area of concern was that Cricket Australia had not given us any attention. We tried on numerous occasions making contact and we even went to the CEO, James Sutherland. We explained the only real communication back from him was via their in house Legal Department!

Both Spotty and I played 1st Grade Cricket, we were both

Australians and HENZ was made in Australia. We really thought that a little bit more Respect was deserved especially as we were mainly trying to Protect Australian Kids. As the Story gathered momentum, I had a horrible feeling inside that our Story may come out in the Paper and Phillip's Parents may read the Article and wonder who were these two blokes trying to "Cash" in on their Son's passing.

HENZ Neck Guard-Protecting Kids.

Being spontaneous, I called directory assistance and asked for the name Hughes in Macksville NSW. To my surprise I was given a phone number and I made the call. A lady answered the phone and I asked "is this Phillip Hughes's Mother?" She paused and said, "Yes". I explained why I phoned and she was very good with her time and said, "the best person to talk to is my Husband Greg". She said, "He is at the farm and call back at 7pm and he will be home by then". I waited till about 7.15 and Mrs Hughes answered again and passed the phone to Greg. He was very good too with his time and after explaining about the contact with the paper he understood why I was concerned and appreciated the call. I said, "Cricket Australia has been very unhelpful" and he told me something that he asked me not to put in the Paper. Out of respect to Greg Hughes I will not write what he said but it was very disappointing what he told me. I asked him if he'd like a HENZ Guard and he was happy to receive one. I didn't make contact again but I felt relieved when the Article came out.

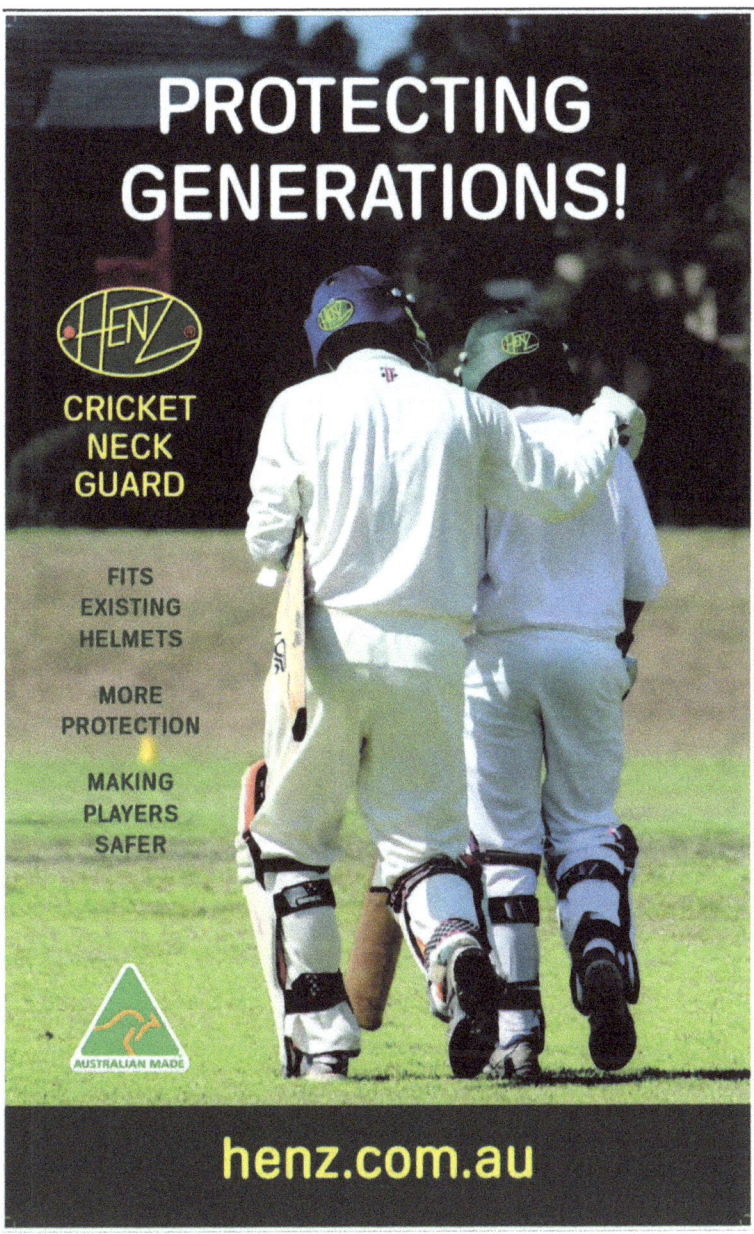

*My most precious "Sporting" picture! The 1st time
Henry and I batted together.It was our "Main"
marketing "Shot" for HENZ, both wearing one.*

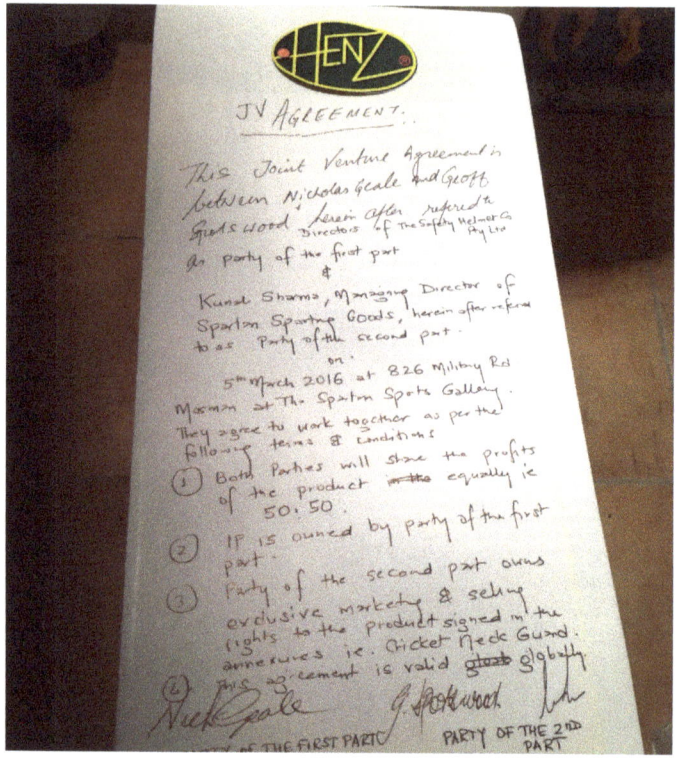

Hand written Contract as a "JV" with Spartan & HENZ.
They pulled out within a week of signing.

We sold to several Sport Shops around Australia but unfortunately there were not many 2nd "Top Ups". What I learnt was it had to be "explained" and the Customer needed it fitted and most Retailer's Staff just turned up and Sold the easy stuff. I reckon I sold over 50 myself when I set up at Kingsgrove Sports Shops. There were a few "Velcro" types on the Market and a definite Competitors version that had Cricket Australia's backing was the Market Leader.

I went to a Sportsman's Night and the brand Spartan was there as one of the Sponsors. I took with me some Marketing material as well as some HENZ guards just in case. I showed the Spartan Representative and he was impressed with HENZ. The very next day we had a meeting with the Owner of Spartan in their Showroom. He showed so much interest he drafted up a Joint Venture, JV on the back of one of our header cards. Spotty and I signed it and we both thought we have just done a massive deal.

Unfortunately the deal was called off less than a week later. I was upset as Henry was with us and he witnessed as Spotty called, Bollywood! The other thing I was "pissed off" about was I met the Owner that afternoon at the Airport and gave him about 6 HENZ guards to take away to India. The Owner is a complete Grub and after talking to a few in the Industry they confirmed my thoughts!

The other area of concern was the Parents were happy to buy a $400 bat for their Child but not spend $35 on Neck Protection! Unfortunately there will be more Incidents and only last Ashes Tour in England, Steve Smith was hit in a similar area.

The HENZ project was another big challenge that I took on. Yes we did not get the Success we were both hoping for. Financially Yes, we lost out but catching up with Spotty more regularly is stuff that money can not Buy. Creating a product and getting it to Market, only a small portion of the Population have done.

Some out there may think it was a Failure, that's fine. I still remember one of Henry's mates Brayden saying very early on when we got HENZ out there, "I got hit on the HENZ today!" Think about those words, who is to know "what if" he didn't have HENZ attached to his helmet?

I put so much Energy and Time into HENZ and yes it definitely had impact on the Business, however I have ZERO regrets.

The Boys and I, Henry far right.

Henry wearing the HENZ Neck Guard So disappointing
Cricket Australia never supported us! Nice Shot H!

ANOTHER TRAGEDY:

It was early evening late April 2015 and as I was heading home from McGraths Hill I heard on the radio there was a Accident in Glenhaven and didn't think any more to it. I was in bed around 8.30 and Daisy bolted into our bedroom in complete distress. She said, "Nathan has been hit by a car and is in a Critical Condition!"

I straight away grabbed my phone and called Uncle Mick. He didn't answer which was so unusual for him and I knew things were serious. I eventually got through to him and the "Gravity" in his voice was so noticeable. He said to me, "not again mate". He was referring to my Brother David's Accident.

The Accident happened directly outside Nathan's home and the circumstances was such a mix up of events. I won't go into details as it is not my place to do so. Nathan was Airlifted to Hospital and the next 24/36 hours must have been horrific for his Family!

Sadly it was decided to turn off his Life Support and unlike my Brother's passing back in the 70's the Family had the opportunity to Donate his Organs and decided to do so. This amazing Gift saved the lives of six people including a baby.

Nathan's Mother asked my Mum months after the Accident, "does it get any easier Elsa?" My Mum replied, "no it doesn't, you just have to keep going forward every day". Both Mothers were a similar age, being in their 40's.

Little Nathan with his Uncle's and Grandad.
His Father is wearing a dark shirt.

50TH BIRTHDAY:

I was so lucky that my Birthday landed on a Saturday night and I decided to have a Party at Sally Place and the Theme was yes, SPORT. Having a Theme is always a laugh and it gets everyone in the mood. I go back to my "Surprise" 40th and the Theme was UK. Amanda dressed up the home in UK areas. Mal next Door wore a "Change of the Guard" outfit, and the funny thing was he is over 6 foot and to add on the hat was nearly 7 foot!

Getting back to my 50th, we set up some "Footy Goal Posts" in the back yard, had a Marquee and being July cranked up a fire. Seeing everyone turn up dressed in Sport was tops. Scotty came as Richy Benaud wearing a wig and holding onto a Microphone that I secured in a Pub one night at the SCG.

I was standing out the back thinking to myself I haven't seen Pricey from Melbourne. It was about 10 minutes later and there was an entourage of people flowing in through the gate. It took me a few seconds to comprehend and it was Pricey and his Missus Jo but others kept coming in. Mikey and Sam, Bruiser and Mandy and Richy and Rebecca! I was so blown away that they all made the effort to come from Melbourne. The atmosphere lifted another 50% and it was Partying from there on!

Come the Speeches, Scotty now Richy Benaud was MC and killed it. He brought up so many good yarns of my times with different people. Bruiser dressed as a Cricketer grabbed the Microphone and wanted to elaborate more about my episode with David Barstow the ex English player. Luckily he kept it under wraps and a good five years later Henry still wants to know what I said to him out in the middle that day.

I use this word quite often "Investing". I have always Invested time with my mates and when there are special moments like half a Century, it's only then you know how important they all are to me!

Luckily Daisy had her 21st at Sally Place too, although it was to be the last Party there which as you read on is a little sad!

My 50th. What a Night! Daisy, Amanda and Henry. 16th July 2016

THE SLIPPERY SLOPE:

It was around 2017 and the Banks were on Notice with the way they were Lending. I was fortunate that I was able to be "Topped Up" without too much hassle previously but those times were soon to change. I knew how much our Home was worth and I knew I was not able to borrow any more, so things were very, very Stressful.

I threw the Dice and Invested on our 3rd Online Shopping cart costing $10,000. I was praying that we may be able to Trade out of things without employing extra Staff? Yes we did have a "Mobile Friendly" Shopping Cart but it just wasn't producing the Sales as I was hoping.

Towards the end of 2018 I went to Melbourne to Celebrate Bruiser's 50th. Although I knew I was not in the Financial position to go, I really needed a small break, albeit 3 days. I went to the City on my own on the Saturday before the Party. It was good not having to talk to anyone for a good 4 hours or so. When you are in Sales and also running your own gig, you are always talking to Customers, Suppliers, Delivery drivers etc and it can be tiring.

I called Foles to see if he was free to catch up but he was taken up with his Basketball. Foles has definitely changed over the Years, I sometimes wish I had the old Rick back but with his kids being disabled has definitely focused all his attention to them. I am so proud of the way he and his Wife Janine have stuck together and devoted their Life to their Children!

I also called Dima but he was heading away for the Weekend. I met Dima through the Foleys as he was going out with Meagan Foley. He is such a Top bloke, always taking the piss and swears like you've never known! He came over to Boyne Hill in the early 90's and mainly played in the 2nds. He did play from memory only one game in the 1st's and it was a funny moment. He was to bowl his first ball in the One's. Because he wasn't that quick I stood up to the stumps. He released the ball and got smacked for six over "Cow Corner" into the swings on the Hill. We both Cracked up and at the end of the Over I said, "welcome to the 1st Team!"

There is another Bloke I have become mates with in Melbourne, his name is Chook. He played Cricket with Mikey, Pricey and Bruiser.

He always comes away on the Ashes Trips and we have lots of beers and laughs. He also supported me with some Electrical bits which I appreciated over the Years.

Melbourne is always a great place to visit and having mates like Foles, Dima, Mikey, Bruiser, Chooka and Pricey means a lot to me.

Roll on Bruiser's Party and it was fantastic seeing everyone and we all had a Great Night! Bruiser is everyone's mate and having him as well as Mikey and Pricey in my life has been special. I stayed at Bruiser and Mandy's that night and woke up hungover.

Pricey black hat, Bruiser the King, Myself and Mikey, all Great Mates.

We all headed out for Lunch before my late flight. As we dropped off Mandy and the Kids, Bruiser and I was on our own trying to find a car park. For some reason I opened up and said, "things are really tough in the Business and I may lose my Home"!

He was really taken back by what I just told him and he felt for me and understood the Gravity of the situation. We had a nice Lunch with Mandy and their two children and it was off to the Airport. We had a few beers and he said, "hang in there mate"!

Bruiser is in a Family Timber Wholesaling Business that his Father started. It has grown with a Turnover of over $200million with a massive Warehouse just built in Sydney as well as similar Size In Melbourne. Unfortunately his Father never witnessed the two New Warehouses as he passed away in his late 50's. Mikey and Pricey too work in the Business.

I mentioned my first Employee Scott previously, He went out on his own with two other guys and I made contact again and started doing Business. I trusted him and I was hoping this may be the Account to get out of our Hole.

The problem when you start dealing with someone "New" is realistically you don't see your first payment until say 45 days if your lucky. In this time they are still ordering gear and Yes you try and keep a lid on how much they order, however it's easier said then done, especially if your desperate.

Things became "quiet" with Communication and this Company owed me around $40,000. There seemed to be a few excuses at to why we were not getting paid but as I said, I trusted Scott. It was around Mid May 2019 and I finally got through to a Site Foreman. I said, "I have been trying to call Scott but I can not get hold of him"? His response was, "you obviously have not heard?" It was there and then I knew Aussie Electrical had run it last Race! They went into Administration owing me $40,000!

I traded with the Builder after directly and only supplied the gear when the funds were deposited into my Bank Account. I also topped up my Margin as I knew the Builder too was under Stress as they needed gear to finish the job.

I drove home that night and went to see my Brother Justin to tell him the bad news. He was obviously disappointed and we discussed the next step. I went home to speak to Amanda indicating things we not good and we may lose everything!

On that weekend I went over to Justin's home and had a meeting with my Cousin David to throw things around. We crunched the Numbers and the Business owed over a Million Dollars to the Bank and Suppliers and that was only a dart hitting the board.

On the Monday, I called my Accountant and it was obvious I needed to see him that evening. At the meeting it was clear I was "done" and left with the horrible thought of telling Amanda.

It was a good 30minute drive and all thoughts were going through my head. I was trying to work out how I am going to come out with the news and I wasn't really sure how Amanda was going to Respond. I started to reminisce about how we built the home and brought the kids up there. It was a horrible 30 minutes and I arrived home around 8.30/9pm.

What made it worse, I entered the Kitchen and Amanda was putting pots into her new drawers as we had a New kitchen installed 6 months previous. Amanda looked at me and I said, "we are done, it's over"! It was very emotional and Amanda took the news better then I thought and she said, "we need to tell the kids"!

They popped down and I said, "I am really sorry but my Business has collapsed and we have to sell our Home"! They were naturally shocked and I said, "I am so sorry, I gave it everything but it just got too hard"! We had a group hug and there were so many tears and it was so so sad and I felt so guilty!

MOVING MOUNTAINS:

My main concern was loosing "Control" of the enormity of the situation. I needed to keep things "Underground" as I didn't want someone like Clipsal or ANZ to close me Up! I wanted to do things under my "Terms" and did not want to go into "Receivership" and in-turn go "Bankrupt"!

We did the normal photo shoot and Marketing and before you knew it there was a Sign up outside the front of 6 Sally Place. We needed to keep things close to us and it was no doubt a shock to our Neighbours of nearly 20 Years.

It was decided to go to Auction rather than a normal Sale Campaign.

We needed a definite Closure Date to pay the Bank and "All" Creditors. Amanda had a friend in the Industry and we went with her.

We were lucky that we didn't need a "Stylist" to do our Home as Amanda has the Flair for keeping it nice. It comes from her Hairdressing and Creative ways. We did Open Homes on the Weekends as well as one in the Week and it was very demanding especially for Amanda. She had to have the home clean and tidy but she took it in her stride!

The Auction date was the last Saturday in June and we went for a 4 Week Settlement as once again I needed to get Funds to everyone that was Owed. I was really Focused in sorting all that was Owed as I wanted to be able to walk down any Street in Australia without anyone saying, "he is the bloke that went Bust & owes you know who".

Anyone that "really" knows me understands that my word is my word and I am not the type of Person who can Rip off Anyone. Yes, it's the harder way of doing it as everything needs settling but Long Term I knew it was the best way.

Sally Place Girls, Marian, Jenny, Amanda, Debbie, Kath.

Neighbours- Dave #9, Pete #5, Danny #10, Mal #8, Me #6, Scotty #1
Missing, Jon #7, Carlos #4, Hulio #3, Raj #2.

I was at the other end, exiting Aussie Electrical and also had to keep things Quiet from both Suppliers and Customers. My first job was to try and get as much good stock back to the Suppliers. I used the excuse, "Times are Tough" and when you send things back to the Suppliers they expect an "order" to the same Value. I was not in the position to do this and the majority of them were supportive.

Next was to start thinking to sell off as many Assets as possible, ie Racking, Forklift, Displays including Home Theatre, Ceiling Fans, anything that was worth something. I was still "Trading" albeit in a smaller way but was not ordering any gear in which hurt. It got to about Mid June and a Customer of mine Mark came in with one of his mate's Johnny who I had met a few times before. I let on what position I was in as I knew they were good blokes and not broadcast things.

They said you need help and next day they delivered a massive empty Shipping Container. I was totally blown away by their Generosity and was so appreciative of it as I knew time was slipping away. To top things off, they even helped out dismantling Racking and all the heavy stuff like Counters etc.

Lifesavers, Big Johnny and Mark with Santa. With these two, "Actions speak louder then Words"! Mates for Life!

Big Johnny turned up with a Shipping Container to store my stuff; he never asked for a Cent!

It was the Wednesday before our Auction and Amanda and I sat down with the Real Estate Girls. At that meeting I disclosed the price we were wanting. I wrote the figure on the back of one of my Business Cards and showed Amanda first. Before the Meeting I said to her, "go with it and everything will be ok". When I put the Business Card on the table the Girls were blown away and their instant reply was "it's too much"! The figure written down was $1,320,000!

There were two main reasons I went for this figure. The main one was I knew $1,300,000 was what I needed to pay off the Bank and Creditors. The 2nd is a bit more involved and an understanding of how Auctions work.

Day after Auction; I miss my Jacaranda Tree!

I have no doubt if there was a "2" in the figure, ie $1,295,000 I was sure in "my" Opinion, the Sell Price may have been less then that. As it turned out we were fortunate to sell it for $1,310,000 which was $10,000 short of my figure but very happy!

We had just over a month to pack up Sally Place and Amanda got onto the job. She decided not to use a normal Removal Company as we didn't really have the spare funds. She came across a Company that drops off small portable storage containers. It worked out to be a really good idea and she started to fill them up each day.

Storage sheds for the move, I think we used 6 all up!

Our "Place" for 19 Years, "Precious" Memories!

Amanda in the Removal Box, she was my "Rock" throughout Our Demise!

Leaving Sally Place was very emotional for all of us but taking down all my Pictures and packing up all my Memories in my Cricket Room was very Sad. Amanda's close mate Nat was there in my room that night and I "finally" broke down! I "sobbed" on her shoulder and said to her, "I am so Sad!" As I am writing this I have "Tears" streaming from my eyes and it's just about two years ago.

I never reached out for anyone for a hand so when Pes called me in the last week and asked if I needed help, I took him up on it. I knew I was running out of time and his Son Cameron who is my God Son, also helped with the heavy stuff. Henry and Cameron worked well together and it was a nice time for them to bond!

They took the washing machine and fridge to Uncle Mick's as we needed them straight away at our New "Rental"! Scotty gave me a hand at Aussie Electrical which I was also so grateful with. Just having him there was just as important as the muscle if I needed a chat. My mate from soccer Sparrow was a Champion and worked so hard with all the crap stuff to do.

Last Family Drinks before leaving Sally Place.

Bradman corner and lastly Steve Waugh Wall (next page).

I was surprised by a visit from Steve in my Buying Group. He asked me if I need any help? I cried as I felt so isolated and totally taken back with him turning up. His Business Partner Raff I got wrong. I was standoffish over the years with him and in the End he made me change my mind. They took as much gear away and paid me Cost! Jimmy another Member also helped out, we go back as far as I was a young Tradesman when he was looking after a big Multinational. Thanks Guys!

In the last week I "Panicked" and took up the offer of one of those Auction Companies to come in and take away anything sellable. Yes I got "Ripped Off" Financially but it was done swiftly and it took away stress as I only had days to clear out Aussie.

On top of this I had to try and find a new job so I put the word out! Because I had a Relationship with Harry at Kingsgrove Sports, I asked if he knew of any Companies looking to hire. He came back to me indicating they had a Managers Position available at their Artarmon Shop. I went for a chat with him and his Wife and I accepted the job and was to start 2nd week in July. It took some pressure off me knowing I had a quick transition rather then a Prolonged one.

Over the Years Suzanne who was there from the Start always said, "I'll be there to turn the lights out in the End"! She was very aware of how we were skating on thin ice. It was a Friday and late afternoon and it was getting to the stage of "Turning" those Lights Off. It was a very "emotional" few minutes and I thanked Suzanne for sticking around till the end!

Scotty and I quite a while back. He is always there for you when you need him!

Suzanne turning out the lights for the last time!

My Soccer Team, Great Blokes.

I mentioned Sparrow from Soccer and I wanted to talk about these Blokes. It was a good 6 or 7 Years ago and I was at Kellyville Park watching Henry or Daisy play. I was walking past Revee who I knew from Cricket and he was with his Soccer Team. For some reason he said, "why don't you play"? I replied, "only position I can play is in Goals". I think he said we need one. I got home and said to Amanda, "why don't I play Soccer"? She said, "why not, you need a release from work". I texted Revee that night and before you knew it I was their Goal Keeper.

It's been such a laugh over the Years, everyone gets the "Piss" taken out of them, Win or Lose! When my Business Imploded I mentioned it to a few of the Boys and two of them, Sparrow and Gazza offered me some money, thinking it will get me back on track. I was so taken back by their Generosity but declined as I indicated it was a hell of a lot Larger than that.

Our last Day at Sally Place!

We go away after every Season to Gazza's Farm and have such a good time. Everyone gets an "Award" and has to "toss" back a "concoction" of not their Choice. My Soccer has helped me get through this tough period and I am so Grateful to be part of such a good bunch of Blokes!

NEW START:

We were very lucky that Uncle Mick gave up his house for us to stay in for a short while after leaving Sally Place. As I have mentioned previously, I have a very close bond with my Uncle. It goes back to my Childhood, Teens and Adulthood. Even when I was away for 10 years in England, I'd call him to see how he was going. Since I returned in the late 90's we'd speak every couple of weeks and recently weekly, sometimes 2 or 3 Times!

As a Nephew it's such a nice feeling knowing how close I am to him. Yes, I sometimes think he will not be around forever and only recently he has had some health issues. I go over to see him as often as I can and have a beer or tea with him and chat about anything. Unfortunately I have not the same relationship with my Nephew Jack and maybe it is because I left to go overseas as he was growing up? When I was growing up, Uncle Mick was always around. Henry too has not such a bond with his Uncle's either, however only recently with Justin doing all the work at #17 they communicate more.

I treasure I am so fortunate but I believe in "Investing". I am not talking about in a Monetary way but an every day, Life Way. As I mentioned to my Kids with the "Gold" Story; if you look after people and are nice to people, good things happen to Good People.

I am blessed to say that I have "Friends" that I know if I was in real trouble they will be there for me. It helps me get to sleep thinking about those Friendships that I have made in England, Melbourne and Sydney. The best part out of all of this is it doesn't cost you anything, only your Time!

The last thing to do was to meet up with my Landlord early Saturday morning. I walked him around and he was happy with all the efforts made in bringing things back to the same as best a possible. He definitely benefited with the New Ceiling in the Showroom and the Extensions upstairs.

As I mentioned I knew Michael from my Tech Days. We were standing near the Roller door with his Girlfriend and the Real Estate Agent who I knew. I opened up and told them where I was at and we "Lost" our Home. It was another Emotional time and I left Unit#1 Groves Ave McGraths Hill for the Last Time!

One of the Last Shots taken, it was a "True" Closing Down Sale!

With just over a week until I was to start at Kingsgrove Sports we booked a Hotel in Kiama and left on Saturday late morning. It was such a nice feeling driving South that everything had been done! One thing I was very aware of was, my "Family" was with me in the car.

We arrived at Kiama and after settling in we all went out to look around. I was keen to go to the Pub and have a Beer and a Punt. Amanda, Daisy and Henry went off Shopping and I went to the RSL. I asked for a Beer and had a few Bets and Won the first couple of Races. It was good Banter with the Locals and eventually Amanda and the kids arrived. We had so much "Fun" that afternoon and it was what we all needed!

Having a Laugh at Kiama, priceless!

The next day we went to see the "Blowhole" which is famous in Kiama. Like always, Henry and I were kicking and passing the Footy. Yes, we may have lost out "Financially" but I am so lucky to have my Family with me! In the Afternoon we went to watch the local Footy and it was such a laugh hanging out with the Locals.

On our way home we went the Coast Road and drove over the Iconic Road that Lapps around the Cliff Face. After that we drove to higher ground and had a Fantastic view of where we had just been. Aussie Electrical was still "bubbling" away but I was not prepared in letting it get in the way of my Family!

Amanda with some Winnings in Kiama, Great Fun!

WORKING FOR SOMEONE ELSE:

Driving to Kingsgrove Head Office for training was very weird. I had been working for myself for over 15 Years and there I was to walk into an Environment and be "Told" what to do. I got through it and started at Artarmon a few days later.

When I arrived at Artarmon after saying hi to the two staff, I walked around the Shop. The thing that stood out mostly was how dirty and run down the place was. I explained to the Staff that I am all about the "Experience" and there was no way our Customers were having a good Experience the way the Shop was. We all got stuck in and cleaned the Shop as well as the Kitchen and Amenities.

We stayed in Uncle Mick's house for about 3 weeks and headed over to #17 Charles St Baulkham Hills.Yes finally I have done the "Full Circle" taking about 52 Years. The house was owned by June and Reece and were Mum and Dad's neighbours since the early 60's. My memories about #17 was going up the front stairs, knocking on their door and June always invited me in and offered me an Ice Cream. At #19 we never had Ice Creams in our freezer so it was a massive treat for me!

Reece was a Pilot for Qantas and they moved away to the UK when their three boys were in their 20's. Unfortunately they too had a Son who was killed in a Car accident, his name was Mark. In later years the eldest Peter, passed away with a Melanoma in his eye. How much bad luck can one Family have!

June and Reece have passed on and Paul the youngest sold their Home to my Brother Justin about 10 years ago for less then $600,000. No one really knew what the Market was going to do over the next 10 years!

They did an upstairs extension in the 80's and the large area was used for June's collection of artefacts from the UK. It also has two Bedrooms as well as a Bathroom and Daisy and Henry slotted in straight away. It was really important for Amanda and I for the kids to be settled as quickly as possible. Having their own area has been good for them to bond closer and yes they have their moments but we both know they are there for each other. Amanda transformed the "House" into a "Home" very quickly and I was lucky to be given a room to make it my "New" Cricket Room.

People ask me sometimes how am I going and I give the "Yeh" ok or Good" but to be honest I wrestle with our "Demise" every single day! The things I notice the most are all the Homes I pass on my way to work and the "For Sale" signs and I know deep down we "Never" will be in the same position as we were!

We chose #17 as Justin needed to do heaps of work on it and having "Outside" Tenants meant no works were able to start. He offered us a good reduction in the "Rent" and about 4 months later work started on a new bathroom. Luckily when it was ripped out Amanda was back in England visiting her Family. COVID gained momentum after she returned and the Bathroom was finish about 4 weeks later. The next "Big Job" as Henry called it was the backyard. The Pool was leaking and Justin decided to fill it in and transform the whole area in readiness for a "Granny Flat".

Granny Flat next to back fence and Lawn above the old pool at #17.

*Dad bought me the Old Man in Wombat
NSW. Willy the other 2. Now in #17.*

I worked at Kingsgrove Sports for nearly Six months and for some reason I reached out to a Customer back in McGraths Hill. I had not been in contact with him and I wanted to let him know about the demise of Aussie Electrical. I met this fella about 10 Years ago when he walked into Aussie Electrical. He was Building a small dwelling near the Hawkesbury River and I found out he was a keen Water Skier. In a discussion he said he sells furniture and as it turned out he is the Major Owner of one of the Largest Furniture Companies in Australia. Over the years I had some meetings with him about my Business and he was aware with the Business stresses I was under. I asked him about his recipe for Success? He replied with, "Leave a Bit on the Table for Everyone".

He came back quite quickly with a text indicating there may be a position at his Company. It was to run their "Clearance Outlet" located in their New Warehouse at Rouse Hill. I was quite interested and being a Family Business I went to have a chat with his Son and the Managing Director. They offered me the Role and took me to have a look at the Clearance Outlet and I went home to think about it and discuss with Amanda.

I took the Job and the thing I have noticed is all the "Stress" I had been under, running my own Business is no longer there. Roll on Dec 2021 and almost 2 Years the Furniture Gig went South. The saying "your a victim of your own Success " applied to me. After 30 Years of Selling I'm done and will go back on the tools and try and re-coup the Losses built up from Aussie Electrical's Demise. See not going Bankrupt has paid off!

GO FUND ME: HAD A CRACK!

I was watching Grand Designs UK one night and as usual the Owner starts to run out of money ¾'s into the job. He casually said, "I will set up a "Go Fund Me" Campaign and pledge for £60,000" yes, nearly $100/125,000! I was hit for six and said stuff this, I reckon I have a more valid reason to start one. So there I was, I had no idea what I was doing and set up my own Campaign named "Had a Crack".

The amount I was pledging was $10,000, why I don't know. I just plucked a figure out of the air and it was only a day or two into it and

I started to get $50, $100 and $200 amounts donated. Next was a combined $1100 from my old Boss who I did my Apprenticeship with and was far too generous!

A few weeks into the Campaign I got a "call" from a young Sparky who I formed a close relationship with at Aussie Electrical. He supported me with my values and didn't like the way 10% was Trading. He and his Wife live with their Parents and when I dropped off a delivery I was always made very welcome. We'd all sit on their back deck over looking the Blue Mountains and had a beer or coffee. I'd talk to his Father about the Horse Races as he loved a small bet and he was always so happy when I arrived.

On the phone call he said to me, "Nick your struggling yeh?" I paused and said "Yes". He said, "we'd like to give you something but you need to come and see us". We arranged an afternoon and on the morning as I was leaving for work, Amanda said "whatever it is take it, don't be difficult!" In the back of my mind I thought maybe a Myers or David Jones voucher?

I arrived and had a few beers as normal and as I was walking out the front to my car, he and his Wife wanted "that" chat. It went from memory something like this and without any names mentioned as I am so respectful to them.

"As you know we go to Canberra to watch the Raiders play and only recently we took a few days off. When we left home we grabbed our "Back Pack" and in it we knew there was a small satchel of "Gold" but we were in such a hurry, we took it with us"

"When we returned from Canberra we were having a late dinner and suddenly we realised we left the satchel of "Gold" and my Wallet on top of the cupboard where we were staying". We both said to each other, "If" we are ever to get back the "Gold" we will give it to someone who needs it more then us"!

It was then he got emotional and took out this little Red Satchel from his top pocket and said, "we'd like you to have this!" I said, "no way" as I was in shock. They both said, "No, we are Religious and you must have it as we don't need it"! I reluctantly took it and later found out it was an "Ounce" and worth approximately $2500!

That evening I sat down Henry and Daisy and went through what happened a few hours before. I wanted them to understand in Life, most go through hurdles and it's out time at the moment. I pulled out the Satchel and from memory handed it to Daisy. They were both bewildered with holding the Gold. I finished with saying if you are "Good" to people along both your "Journey's", "Good" things happen to "Good" people.

Not long after this I got a phone call from a mate who I met through Daisy's Soccer. Graham also got my text and said, "I am a bit unsure of "Go Fund Me" but send me your Bank Account details and I'll send you a Bone". I just thought he'd put $100 in but he put 3 x $500 over a 3 month period.

On the "Flip Side", I sent my "Go Fund Me" text to the Owner of a well known Plumbing Supplier in Sydney. The reason I sent it to him was my Brother Justin's Company who has a Turnover of Approx $50/55 Million is his "Biggest" Customer! I also know him and helped "facilitate" the purchase of the vacant land next to Aussie Electrical where he built a New Warehouse to service the Hawkesbury.

I thought maybe, he may find a couple of "Bucks" in his pocket? I got a quick text back from him with the words "Hang On!" To be honest, I took it as hang on and I'll get back to you. I was wrong and never heard anything else.

I really don't care that he didn't donate anything or maybe he did an "Anonymous" Donation. I just thought his text with "only" two words may have been a bit more considerate. My text clearly read "I Closed my Business and had to Sell our Home to pay off all Debts and now Renting"! He may use the "Excuse" he was busy and rushed his Reply? Poor form.

PARENTS:

Mum and Dad had been Married for over 60 Years and they had let's say an interesting Marriage. They definitely went through tough times loosing their Son but somehow they came out the other side.

Mum was Extraverted where Dad was the Opposite, however they got on and were Great Parents to us Boys. In Later Years they were to become Grandparents and spoilt the Grandkids not just with Presents but their Time! Mum loved taking the kids to the Movies and Dad loved playing with any Toys either made or purchased at the Markets.

They moved into a Nursing Home just before Mum's 80th Birthday. This was all very Stressful as Mum was certain that she'd never move out of #19. Justin was instrumental in finding such a great Home for them to move into.

Unfortunately they both had become very immobile. Mum suffered from Arthritis and was in pain towards her later Years. Dad suffers from Osteoarthritis and as I have mentioned he has Dementia as well.

Unfortunately Mum was Diagnosed with Bowel Cancer just short of 2 years after she moved into the Nursing Home and she decided not to have Chemotherapy. Mum sadly lost the "Battle" and Passed Away in June 2020.

I miss going to see her and just chat about anything. She had the ability to make anyone comfortable in her surrounds. This may be someone she has known all her life or someone she had just met on any given day.

Dad was always out the back in the Family Room normally watching UK Comedy. His favourite was Mrs Bucket or Mrs "Bookah" as she pronounced it. You'd hear his laughing from outside the house!

As I write this, Dad is in his 89th Year and I visit him as much as I can. Sometimes he knows who I am and sometimes he doesn't. For a person who gave out so much "knowledge" it seems unfair his "Mind" has gone!

Great Parents to us. Justin in Blue, Anthony in Pink. Dad never showed too much Affection to Mum in Public, this is about it! Love this Pic, sadly one Person Missing!

#19's Lounge Room. Mum loved Art, Books and "Out There" Sculptures. Christmas Day. Justin, Kathy, Emily, Hannah, Anthony, Uncle Mick, Amanda, Daisy, Henry. Missing Jack, Jessica.

*Taken at Christmas. Mum and Dad moved out to a Nursing
Home a few Years Later. Sadly Dad passed 1st Feb 2022.*

*Everyone has Great Photos of their Parents, I came
across this one in concluding my Story. Dad 29, Mum
24. Thanks Mum and Dad! Love Nick*

LAST SESSION:

Anyone who has played or watched a Test match knows there is the last Session on Day 5. Sometimes it ultimately ends in a Draw or on some Occasions there is a Winning Team. We are now in that Last Session and I'd like to think the next few Paragraphs indicate a Winner.

Sometimes words are not needed!

Amanda and I were given a bottle of Champagne from Peter and Marian across the Road at Sally Place as a "Leaving Gift". Peter is a big collector of Wines and always keen to share some of them with you. We knew the Champagne was "Top Shelf" and we wanted to save it for a "Special Occasion". In the January holidays just gone, Amanda and I went on a Road Trip. We stayed at Graham and Sandra's home in Coffs Harbour who Donated those 3 amounts to my Campaign. We Celebrated their "generosity" with the Champagne. They both were extremely grateful we chose them to share it with.

I think it was the next day and we were all having a walk near the Harbour. I asked Graham, "have you got any advice for me on my next Stage in Life"? I was expecting him to come back with ideas on Investing your Inheritance or something similar? He came back with, "If I was you, I'd cuddle your Wife and Kids each day"!

Thanks Amanda x

STUMPS!

*Celebrating the arrival of my Sample Copy with my
Late Father's portrait in background.*